I  SUBURBIA

I ♥ SUBURBIA

The Joys of Life on London's Outskirts

SIMON POLLOCK

CONTENTS

	INTRODUCTION	6
PART 1 /	IF YOU BUILD IT, THEY WILL COME	10
	Here Come the Trains	12
	Roadside Icons	38
PART 2 /	THE GREAT EXPANSION	96
	From Houses to Homes	98
	Flats: Going Up in the World	128
	Suburban Institutions	150
PART 3 /	LIVING THE (SUBURBAN) LIFE	168
	Old Buildings, New Uses	170
	Suburban Oddities	202
PART 4 /	DAYS OUT OF THE SUBURBS	220
	Road Trip, Anyone?	222
	AND THAT'S A WRAP	250
	A BIG THANK-YOU FROM ME	252
	WANT TO EXPLORE SUBURBIA MORE?	253

INTRODUCTION

Like many readers of this book, I was born in the suburbs. I didn't choose to be – if I'd had my way, I would have been born somewhere a lot cooler, maybe a penthouse in Paris or the mean streets of New York City. My parents would have been astronauts or racing drivers – but they weren't, they were a civil servant and a school secretary. So, instead of spending my life jetting around the world watching spaceship launches and motor races, I watched them happen on our big boxy TV, from our floral-patterned sofa that sat on the floral-patterned carpet, hidden behind net curtains in a house that looked like every other house on the outskirts of London.

That's not to say that life was boring. I had a great childhood with loving parents: we had a treehouse in the garden, a cinema around the corner, and every summer we'd pack the car up and drive to the English coast, to somewhere exotic like Bournemouth or Bognor. Life was comfortable – and safe.

So, like many a teenager before me, I moved out of suburbia to spend my twenties and thirties in more 'interesting' places. I travelled the world, I got into extreme sports, I met new people and I lived the life that I felt suburbia had denied me. It was only when my first daughter was on her way that I reluctantly moved back. And to my surprise, things looked different this time around.

The first thing I noticed was that no two houses looked exactly the same. Sure, when they were built they were carbon copies of each other, but when you looked again there was evidence that decades of different owners had made small changes. Some houses had window frames made of wood, some were plastic and yet others were metal. There were mismatched loft extensions on adjoining semi-detached houses, and concrete driveways sat next to flower gardens, exotic palm trees competing with silver birch. There were clues to the personalities and tastes of past and present residents in the outward appearance of almost every house. Everything had been customised; everything was different.

The next thing that struck me was how some of the buildings made me feel. Train stations dotted about were reminders of happy days out as a child, and certain buildings near where I grew up brought back memories of long car rides home, when spotting them meant we were almost there. When I saw the old Gillette Factory for the first time in decades, I was transported back to a car journey in the 1970s: I'd spent that entire drive looking out of the back window in awe of all the decorated Christmas trees in front of the old art deco factories.

Once I started to look around properly, it quickly became apparent to me that the suburbs are an architectural wonderland. The creation of the greater part of London's suburbs in the 1930s had coincided with the interwar modernist architectural movement, bringing for the first time more 'avant-garde' designs to Britain – buildings designed with a mix of clean lines, geometric symmetry and elegant simplicity.

We've all seen photos of London's architectural gems: St Paul's, the Houses of Parliament, the Barbican – the list goes on. But how many of us have marvelled at the beauty of a factory in Brentford, or the town hall in Walthamstow, or the magnificent Hoover Factory on the A40? All around the outer boroughs of London, there are stunning examples of factories, town halls, private houses, blocks of flats, cinemas and stations that wouldn't be out of place in Miami Beach. These truly are masterpieces, but because they're in Southgate, Ruislip, Forest Gate or Surbiton, they don't get the recognition they deserve.

So, in March 2022, I decided to set up an Instagram account, @LondonSuburbia. I wanted to see what would happen if I shared some pictures of old suburban buildings on a platform more famous for showcasing beautiful people pretending to live the high life in far-off locations. Armed with my second-hand camera, I uploaded five pictures with some straightforward text about the architectural history of some of the buildings and continued to add a picture a day for a month or so.

A few people began to follow the account, but writing the architectural text was, well, dull. One night, I wrote a piece about how I'd gone to see Santa as a child in Bentalls, Kingston. To my surprise, people began to comment, sharing their memories in response. It took a few more posts before the penny dropped and I realised that it wasn't only the buildings that were important, it was what they meant to people. The memories that people had of those places and what they used to do in and around them – that was what people wanted to read about.

And that, dear reader, is what this book is all about: looking at the biggest part of any city, its suburbs, with fresh eyes. As I live on the outskirts of London, what follows is a tour of that city – with some forays beyond.

Of course, you might disagree with me about my definition of suburbia, which sort of begins in Zone 2 of the London Underground and stretches about ten miles outwards towards the M25, but I hope I'll persuade you why Camden's gems can be just as overlooked or underappreciated as those of Brentford. And the truth is, I try not to get too hung up on what we call suburbia – because it's always changing. If you asked a historian, they'd probably tell you that everywhere outside of the original Roman city walls was at one time suburban, depending on what year you visited, but I don't think many people these days consider places like Soho and Westminster to be the suburbs.

Ultimately, this isn't really a book about architecture, nor is it a book about photographs of architecture. This is also not the kind of book that will show you an old cinema and tell you who designed it and which school of design the architect got their inspiration from. This is a love letter to suburbia, the people who live there and those that built it for us.

I hope you enjoy looking at the pictures, reading the stories behind some of the iconic buildings and hearing the memories and tales of the amazing people who grew up there.

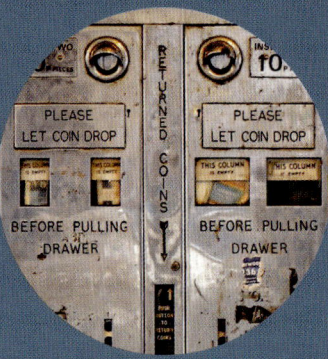

PART 1

IF YOU BUILD IT, THEY WILL COME

HERE COME THE TRAINS

When we think about suburbia, what often comes to mind are wide, grass-verged roads, family SUVs sitting on driveways, and rows of almost identical semi-detached houses with small front lawns that get mown every Sunday. The outskirts of London are home to this stereotypical suburban lifestyle, and new estates are going up all the time – often on reclaimed industrial sites or in pockets of undeveloped land between suburbs.

But where did the suburbs come from? Much of suburbia has its roots in the mid nineteenth century, when the rail network was first invented. This new technology brought out-of-city living to the middle class, and for the first time allowed working men and women to commute to work from railway suburbs like Surbiton, Richmond and Chiswick.

But if you've ever wondered why we tend to associate the suburbs with rows of 1930s semis, the answer lies in the twenty or so years between the two world wars when London felt good about itself. Buoyed by post-war optimism, the government handed out large subsidies to encourage low-density building – first to councils and later to private property developers. 'If you build it, they will come' became the mantra of rail companies everywhere, as they rapidly built new stations in relatively unpopulated countryside to provide fast transport into the centre of London, and around these new stations, new suburbs sprang up. Soon, life on the outskirts became an aspiration and top architects were employed to convey all the positive feelings of the day, inspired by the best in modern architecture from Europe.

So let's begin our celebration of suburbia with the stations that made it possible – from the stations that enabled the great expansion of London to the architectural gems that opened up a new world of design

CLAPHAM COMMON

It's a suburb, I promise! Or at least Clapham Common was a suburb back when this cute and curvy station was built in the 1920s to replace the original late-Victorian one.

Though it might not be considered part of the suburbs today, Clapham Common is the perfect station to start our journey because it was the first complete station that the architect Charles Holden designed, and it opened in 1924. He was employed by Frank Pick, the boss of the Underground Electric Railways Company of London, to bring new and modern designs to the network – and you may well have heard of Mr Holden as he had a hand in designing most of London's coolest Tube stations in the 1920s and 1930s. It's fair to say that he ended up as a bit of a legend because of it and has won the highest of British honours: a pub named after him.

For twenty years or so before Clapham Common was built, the most up-to-date Tube designs in London tended to be covered in shiny red ceramic tiles, often with very elaborate tiled interiors too (think Camden Town, Mornington Crescent or Edgware Road). But once Holden and Pick decided to modernise, this kind of riff on the English version of art nouveau – an architectural style famous for its organic flowing curves and the influences of nature – emerged, leaving Clapham with a beautiful landmark. The way Holden and Pick interpreted modernism and the designs they produced would soon radically change, so this experimental little station is very much a visual marker of the end of the old and the start of the new.

Today Clapham Common Station is teeming with young professionals commuting to and from work and it's not for the faint of heart. Down below it's got one of the narrowest and scariest 'island' platforms on the network – so not only do people have to queue outside the station at rush hour, as

the platform isn't big enough to fit everyone trying to get in, but those lucky enough to be crammed inside are forced to wait inches from a thundering Tube train. Some would say it's a pain, but others might argue a bit of adrenaline is the perfect way to wake up In the morning. At any rate, it's a lot cheaper than buying a coffee in Clapham, I can tell you.

MORDEN

It's hard to imagine today, but when Morden Station was built, it sat in the middle of nowhere, surrounded by farmland and wide, open fields. The station was built in 1926 as the southern terminus for the Northern Line extension (which started from Clapham Common) and the area grew ninefold in just ten years after the station arrived. The concrete facade is original to the station and there's a pretty good story behind why it's not the greatest looker.

Shortly after Clapham Common was built, Frank Pick – the boss of the network – was eager to build stations with ultra-modern designs. Modernism (or 'art deco' as we colloquially call it today) was becoming all the rage in Europe, and Pick wanted to bring those designs to London. His grand vision was to build stations in reinforced concrete with as little ornamentation as possible. (Sounds lovely, right?)

And so the age of modernism on the London Underground began. From Clapham Common to Morden, all the stations along this extension of the Northern Line were built in a similar, stripped-back style. But it's incredible to see how much difference there is between Clapham Common and Morden, when they were only built two years apart. And it's funny to think how the way we view design has changed too. Today, art deco tends to be used to describe the more avant-garde designs of the 1920s and 1930s, but it was only in the 1960s that this term first appeared in print and really became popular. Architectural scholars like to argue long and hard about what *is* art deco (or streamline moderne or simply modernist!) but the truth is that most cool buildings are a mix of all sorts of styles.

If you want to impress your friends with your design-history nous, though, art deco architecture tends to be boxy, with strong vertical lines; streamline moderne tends to have a more horizontal feel, with organic curvy lines; and modernist, well, that tends to be stripped down, with minimal ornamentation – although, just to confuse matters further, art deco and streamline moderne are usually considered to be types of modernism. But I really don't think it matters. It's like arguing about what musical genre a song belongs to rather than just asking, 'Do I like this song?' I try not to get too hung up on it, and focus more instead on whether I like the look of a building or not.

RAYNERS LANE

After the harsh-looking concrete boxes of the Morden extension, things started to relax a bit when Charles Holden and his colleague Stanley Heaps came up with the most prolific 1930s design found on the Underground network: the brick box with windows. Stations like Rayners Lane can be found all over London and are deceivingly big on the inside. From the outside, they look like a multistorey building, but on the inside, they're more like a suburban cathedral – one big room with huge windows stretching from floor to ceiling.

The stations from this era can vary a bit in design but they often have lovely intricate art deco details, curvy wooden ticket booths – and bewildered pigeons trying to work out what on earth they've flown into. If you look closely, too, you can see some curves starting to creep back in – check out those little shops underneath the Underground signs.

BOSTON MANOR & OSTERLEY

Of course, not all stations on the network built in the 1930s followed the same formula, and there are some very striking ones dotted about, born of a more fun day at work for the architects, I suspect. I absolutely love the stations at Boston Manor and Osterley for their bold and unexpected design. They were built at the same time and share similar quirks because they were both designed by Stanley Heaps, head architect at the Underground Electric Railways Company of London, with help from Charles Holden.

Besides Frank Pick, I can't think of anyone else who's had a bigger influence on London's Tube design than these two, who began working together just after the end of the First World War and were hugely inspired by European modernist architecture. Throughout the interwar years, as London started to get back on its feet, Heaps and Holden would travel abroad to study these ultra-modern, elegant designs and find ways to incorporate elements from them into their own work.

But although modernist designs are all about simplicity and a lack of ornamentation and fussy details, by the time Holden and Heaps designed these stations in 1934 that was starting to change, hence the illuminated futuristic flourishes that you can see here in the obelisks on top of the buildings.

Fun fact: the obelisk on top of Osterley is said to be based on the one on De Telegraaf building in Amsterdam, and if you search for an image of it online, you will see Osterley's is almost a carbon copy!

21

SOUTHGATE

Opened in 1933, Southgate Station is a perfectly round building stacked full of features you don't see anywhere else. It's unique so I'm not really sure what architectural box you could put it in – maybe art deco? Or streamline moderne? Or possibly Martian spaceship?

It was extensively modernised in 1980 and 2008, with works carried out to maintain the art deco interior features of the original station – such as the brass uplighters and bronze panelling.

Southgate is a busy and vibrant place to visit, and a great example of how buildings can be preserved. The station is Grade II* listed, which means that it's a nationally protected historic building and that every effort will be made to preserve it. It also means that Southgate Station is in the top 10 per cent of listed buildings in the UK. The exceptional level of care this station has received can be seen in details like the escalators, which have been replaced using bronze rather than the standard London Transport aluminium.

Southgate is one of the most loved gems of the London transport network, and yes, that space-age stack of pancakes on top does light up at night.

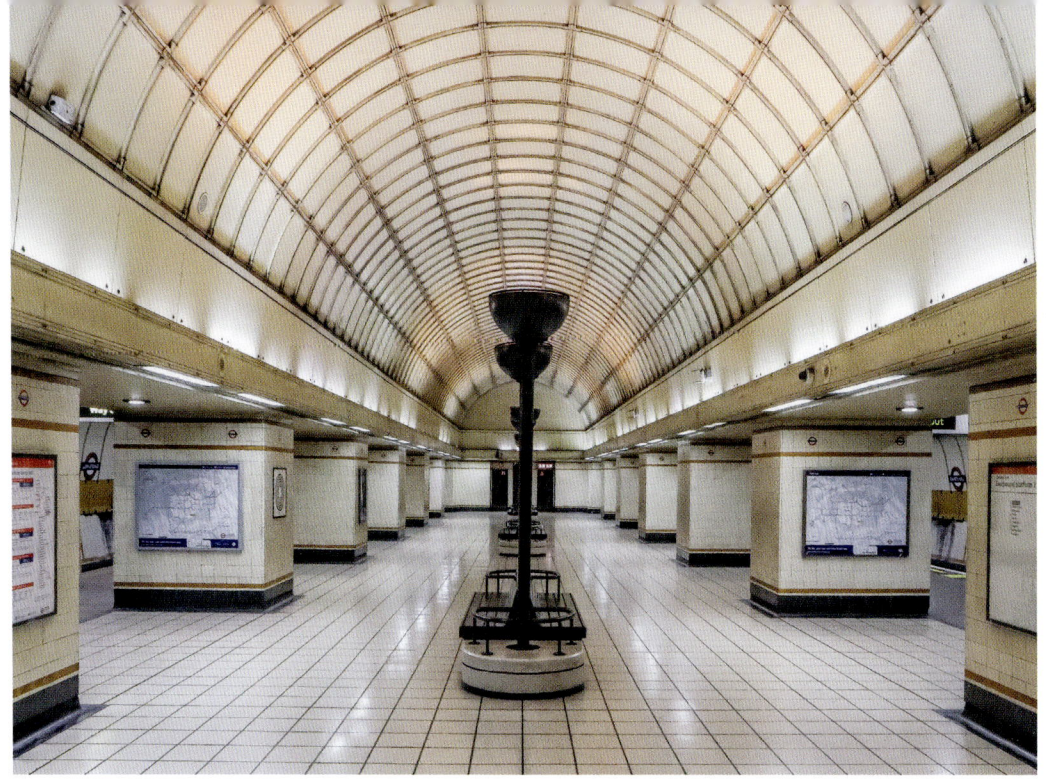

GANTS HILL

The vaulted hall at Gants Hill Station is wonderful and probably the only part of the Underground where I would actually choose to sit and relax for a bit, enjoy the scenery and let a few trains go by. Rumour has it that the station's architect – and our familiar friend – Charles Holden met with the designers of the Moscow Metro before the war, so either Gants Hill was inspired by the Moscow Metro or the Moscow Metro was inspired by Gants Hill. I like to think it was the latter, but don't quote me on that.

CHISWICK PARK

Built in 1932, this is another classic Holden–Heaps collaboration – this time inspired by the Krumme Lanke metro station in Berlin. With its pleasing organic curves packed full of windows that let light pour into the main ticket hall, it's a brilliant example of the modernist philosophy of keeping design straightforward and elegant. It's so simple that a child could have drawn it, yet so confident and well executed that it's always a welcome sight on a daily commute. It's easy to see why both stations are so cherished by their home cities, with the station in Berlin being rebuilt in 1989 to its original design, and Chiswick Park being listed as a Grade II building.

UXBRIDGE

Uxbridge station is pretty cool, isn't it? It's one of those places in suburbia that's really worth taking some time to look at. In fact, if it were more socially acceptable, I'd be sitting outside in a camping chair most days with a Thermos of tea, staring at it.

It was built in 1938 and went through a number of design iterations before this one was agreed. Charles Holden's original sketch for the station was very grand, but after he did the drawing, he passed the design over to some subcontracting architects to finish as he was rather busy at the time with all the other work flooding in from the London Underground. What they came back with was somewhat more traditional-looking and not to the liking of Holden's boss, Frank Pick, who instructed Holden to take control of the work again in what sounds like a loud and direct conversation involving the potential loss of his employment. The result was the magnificent cathedral-like station that you see here, with a few additional features intended to express speed and modernity.

Holden did cut a few corners though, as the whole platform area is a cut-and-paste of Cockfosters Station's, about forty-five stops away. There is no record of whether Holden had to endure another shouting session from Frank Pick for this, but it was a very prolific time for suburban London station building and who can blame him for taking a few shortcuts.

LITTLE DETAILS EVERYWHERE

The London Underground network today is truly amazing: there are so many small things dotted around that haven't been used for years but are still there and look like they did when they were first built. I love that about the Tube. I don't think it's neglect but a reverence for the past that means these details have been preserved.

Writing this book has taught me to spend time properly seeing the things around me – and after years of commuting with my face stuck in my phone, it has been heart-warming to notice the nineteenth-century tiles, 1930s brass uplighters, and original station names peeking through layers of paint.

I can't recommend it enough. If you're reading this book on a Tube train, why not put it down and look up?

(If you can't put this book down though – and who can blame you – here are a couple of my personal favourite little details, at least one of which has appeared on a previous page. Did you spot it?)

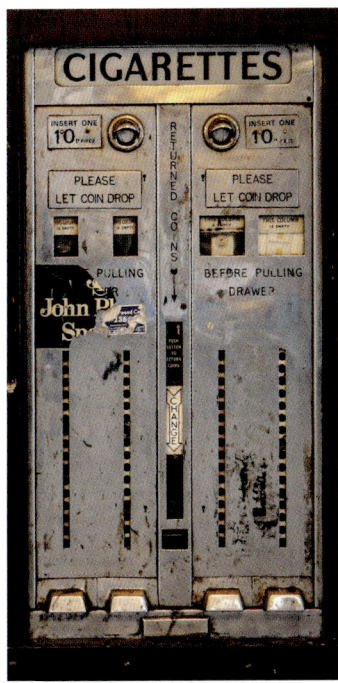

EAST FINCHLEY

'Archie', *The Archer*, was completed in 1940 by celebrated sculptor Eric Aumonier, who was known for his art deco reliefs on cinemas and ultra-modern 1930s buildings. Made of six hundredweight of beechwood, wrapped in lead with gilded accents and finished with an ash bow coated in copper and gold, the ten-foot sculpture sits on the roof of East Finchley station on the Northern Line, the longest Underground tunnel built in Europe at the time. In an age of great technological advancement, Archie was a metaphor for the incredible speed with which the trains ran, and he faces in the direction of Morden, all the way at the other end of the line.

Although much loved now, Archie was controversial back in the day. In 1940, the *Hendon and Finchley Times & Guardian* published a strongly worded editorial stating their dissatisfaction that it wasn't a statue of the local hero and eighteenth-century highwayman, Dick Turpin (who was neither a local nor a hero, by the way!).

Wouldn't it be fun if there were a giant arrow placed at Morden on the other end of that thirteen-mile tunnel?

THE ART DECO LINE
MOTSPUR PARK TO CHESSINGTON SOUTH

London is not all about the Underground network, of course, and in South London there's a very unusual Overground line indeed. It's a small branch line, with just four stations after Motspur Park – Malden Manor, Tolworth, Chessington North and Chessington South – and each of them is designed in an art deco style.

Originally opened in 1939, the line was built to relieve traffic on a parallel part of the network. But of course, in 1939 Britain entered the Second World War, and at that point only four of the stations had been built.

Construction was slow to get going after the war, and by the time it was ready to start up again the green belt had been introduced in an Act of Parliament to limit the growth of the city. The remaining part of the line was never completed, so the line terminated at Chessington South.

Each station was designed by James Robb Scott, the chief architect at Southern Railways, who also designed the very grand Victory Arch at Waterloo as well as my favourite Overground station at nearby Surbiton. In the 1930s, he designed a host of other art deco stations dotted around the Southern Railways network, his last being the unexpected terminus of this branch line at Chessington South.

Fun fact: while each station has a lift shaft, the lifts were never installed, leaving a pointless tower at each station.

SURBITON

To my mind, the jewel in the crown of the Overground network is Surbiton; it really stands out for me as the finest example of an art deco station in London. It's the gift that keeps on giving, too, as it has not one but two superb deco entrances, a matching clock tower and even perfectly preserved 1930s waiting rooms on the platforms, with curved glass nestling in their original steel frames. What's not to love? The first station was built here in 1838 and was replaced by the current version in 1937.

Before it was renamed Surbiton Station in 1867 it was called Surbiton and Kingston. Before that it was called Kingston Junction, and before *that* Kingston, which was ironic because in 1838 it was located in some fields near the small hamlet of Surbiton, almost two miles away from the nearest town of Kingston itself. Why was such an important station stuck miles away from the bustling market town it claimed to serve? Well, at the time, Kingston Corporation (the council) feared that a newfangled railway would steal trade from their coaching business, so they objected to its construction. How right they were! Their only miscalculation was exactly how much the railway would change the area.

With the arrival of the station and its direct trains to London, Surbiton experienced a huge housing and economic boom, and to this day is still a major suburb. Some thirty years later, Kingston Council realised they had made a big mistake (took them long enough!) and a Kingston Station was eventually opened in the town. The last laugh went to Surbiton though, as Kingston was placed on a small branch line with slow trains to London, while Surbiton became a major hub on the network. By 2014 the country's most overcrowded train was the 8.04 a.m. from Surbiton to London Waterloo, and its equivalent today is still in the top ten nationally.

ROADSIDE ICONS

During the great suburban expansion of the 1920s and 1930s, hundreds of miles of roads were built around the outskirts of London to ease congestion. Roads like the North Circular, the Western Avenue and the Great Cambridge Road allowed people to speed around the city in their state-of-the-art automobiles, which generally made visiting friends, taking day trips and, of course, commuting to and from work all much easier.

These new roads were connected by huge arterial highways and, very quickly, factories, housing estates, warehouses and offices all sprang up alongside them, as did the infrastructure to support motorists, such as petrol stations, cafes and hotels.

These familiar roadside buildings have become personal waymarkers for Londoners, letting us know we're nearly home or reminding us of a cherished childhood trip out of the city in Mum and Dad's car. And thankfully, although we've lost a huge amount of our industrial past over the years to demolition and development, a lot of these buildings have since become subject to preservation orders. There are some stunning examples dotted around these now packed routes, and further out in the commuter towns too.

When so many of the buildings I grew up with are now long gone, it's reassuring to drive past one that's still there and to enjoy the warm feeling of seeing an old friend – albeit one that never phones, always forgets my birthday and didn't turn up to my wedding.

THE COMET HOTEL
Hatfield, AL10 9RH

This rather splendid building is the Comet Hotel in Hatfield. It sits a few miles north of London's orbital traffic jam, the M25, and was designed by E. B. Musman. Completed in 1936 in a streamline moderne style, it features sweeping horizontal lines and sexy curved brick and glass, kind of like an ocean liner.

The hotel is named after the de Havilland DH88 Comet aircraft, which was built in a local factory about half a mile away – and that red aeroplane you see on top of the white pole is a model of the aircraft itself. Cool, isn't it?

The Comet Hotel started off as a roadhouse on the newly designated A1 and was essentially an early version of the motorway service station. Roadhouses sprouted in prime locations on new roads and were often owned by breweries – as was the Comet. The architect of this one, however, didn't want to restrict himself to the term 'roadhouse' and claimed it was a 'hotel, cocktail lounge, tea room, dance hall, sports facility, roadhouse and public house', which never really seemed to catch on.

It's just undergone a huge refurbishment and looks absolutely spiffing. And now that the building is firmly a hotel and past the identity crisis its designer gave it, it's the perfect place to pop out for a 1930s dry martini.

ACE CAFE
Wembley, NW10 7UD

The legendary Ace Cafe in Wembley has been a hangout for motorcyclists and petrolheads since it was built in 1938. Originally a small service stop for motorists travelling on the North Circular, it featured a petrol station, a cafe and the UK's first automated car wash.

In 1940 it was all but destroyed by a stray wartime bomb, but reopened in a temporary wooden building until 1949 when it was rebuilt in the form you see today.

When teenagers were invented in the 1950s (or so my dad tells me), the cafe became a mecca for young people as it was one of the few places you could listen to rock 'n' roll on a jukebox.

Motorcycle-based subcultures like the Ton-Up-Boys and the Rockers gravitated to the cafe, which provided a safe haven where they could hang out with like-minded people over a cup of tea.

'Cafe racing' originated in places like the Ace, where 'record races' would take place. The rules were simple: put a coin in the jukebox, get on your bike, race around a defined road route and return to the cafe before the song finished.

The cafe closed its doors in 1969 and eventually a tyre-fitting business moved in. Twenty-five years later, in 1994, an Ace Cafe reunion was organised, meeting on the forecourt of the tyre company. To say it was a success is an understatement: 12,000 bikers turned up. The event continued annually, which led to the organisers buying the freehold to the building and reopening it as the Ace Cafe in 2001, with the exterior fully restored to the spec of the 1949

art deco building. The rest, as they say, is history, and the Ace Cafe is once again a mecca for bikers and petrolheads.

If you wanted to do the record-racer route in a car today, it would take around twelve minutes – and that's if you're lucky with the lights. A song this long might really upset the patrons. Not recommended.

EAST SHEEN FILLING STATION
East Sheen, SW14 7ED

This small filling station in East Sheen dates back to 1926 and is one of the earliest surviving petrol stations in the UK. At the time, filling stations were often little more than a shed, some roadside pumps and maybe an advertising sign, but as the countryside turned into the suburbs, money flowed in and bijou country-lane petrol stations started to invest in their appearance.

Operated by the long-gone Blue Star group, this filling station was placed on a stretch of road between orchards and small farms that soon became part of the quickly expanding suburbs. Its design is inspired by American filling stations, with an integrated canopy and office configuration that's now familiar around the world.

It's quite eye-catching and easy to get a good look at when you're inevitably stuck in a traffic jam on the heavily congested Upper Richmond Road. As a Grade II listed building, much like the cars nearby it's not going anywhere any time soon.

A WALK DOWN THE GOLDEN MILE
Brentford

Without a doubt, the highest concentration of large-scale 1930s industrial buildings on any of London's arterial roads can be found in Brentford on a stretch of the Great West Road between Chiswick and Syon Lane. Locally referred to as the Golden Mile, it was so named due to the huge amount of industry situated along a relatively short distance of road.

But having a bunch of factories along a road doesn't really merit the word 'golden', does it? Well, what sets this mile of factories and warehouses apart is the way the factories were built, often showcasing the latest art deco styles in a sort of corporate one-upmanship, each new one trying to outdo the last in a peacock-like show of grandeur. The chief executives who commissioned those factories back in the 1920s and 1930s were probably overcompensating for something, but at least they weren't making a global menace of themselves as others were doing at the time!

A lot of the glorious factories of the Golden Mile are long gone, but there are still some left in first-class condition. What's more, these days – in a strange twist of fate – developers are fitting these buildings out with fancy apartments and cool office spaces. These buildings used to be knocked down without a thought and replaced with modern housing, but developers have realised that a lot of people dream of living and working in a converted art deco factory. Good news all round, I say.

It's easy enough to get to the Golden Mile to see all these buildings: from the west, drivers can park in one of the car parks provided by out-of-town retailers or take the train to Syon Lane and start there. From the east, you can get the train to Brentford and work your way westwards, starting at Wallis House.

It's not the most peaceful of walks as it's along a busy road, but it certainly is free food for the soul and good exercise.

WALLIS HOUSE

Wallis House is at the eastern, Chiswick end of the Golden Mile and about a ten-minute walk from Brentford Station. It's well worth the effort to stroll past the building, as it's difficult to appreciate on a drive-by since it's mostly obscured by a huge flyover. It was designed by Wallis, Gilbert and Partners in 1937 and the first owner was Simmonds Aerocessories, which made parts for aeroplanes. Over the years the building has had a number of tenants, including SmithKline Beecham, which famously applied to demolish it in 1996, wanting to replace it with a new development by superstar architect Richard Rogers.

A big kerfuffle followed, with strong arguments on both sides for either preserving it or replacing it with fashionable new buildings, until the council stepped in and said, 'Guys, why don't we preserve it and put new buildings round the back?'

Since then, the original building has been listed for preservation and converted into apartments and offices. To this day it remains an icon to Londoners on their way in and out of West London.

CURRYS DISTRIBUTION CENTRE

If you wander west from Wallis House, this is the first art deco building you will come across. It is currently owned by JCDecaux (the street furniture people), but it started life as a distribution centre and head office for Currys. Currys is now a household name in electronics, but back then it sold a mix of bicycles, toys and radios.

The warehouse opened in 1936 at a key moment in Currys' history, when it began to transition from primarily selling bicycles to electronics. As a result of that, in 1936 the Currys' newspaper adverts are more than a little confusing as they simultaneously try to sell teddy bears, bicycles, vacuum cleaners, work overalls, radios, car indicators, wellington boots and accordions. What sort of company does that? Hang on, that sounds like the middle aisle of Lidl, doesn't it?

PYRENE FACTORY

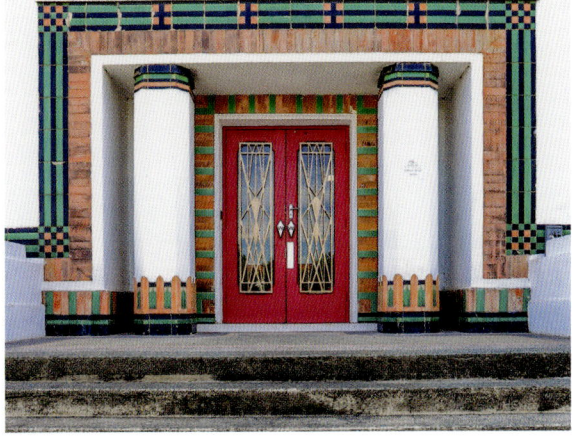

Next up on our little walk is the Pyrene Factory, built in 1930 and designed by Wallis, Gilbert and Partners (sound familiar?).

Pyrene was a fire extinguisher company which had a sense of showmanship. Behind the factory, it had a large demonstration ground where it could simulate oil depot fires to showcase its products in action. When the site opened, the company even managed to get the opening shown in cinemas: if you want a delightful trip back in time, it's worth searching online for *Pyrene Factory opened in Brentford*.

Back in the day, Pyrene wasn't the only art deco fire extinguisher factory in the area – the Minimax Factory was just down the road in Feltham. Incidentally, Pyrene purchased Minimax in 1955 – and you can see what's left of the latter factory in the Oddities section of this book (page 212).

Who'd have thought the fire suppression business would build such grand factories, eh?

THE FIRESTONE FACTORY

Opposite the Pyrene Factory there are a wall, some lights and a pair of old gates. They're all that's left of the once palatial 1930s Firestone Tyres Factory, and unusually, they're all listed for protection.

Why, you ask? Well, in its heyday, an iconic factory designed by the prolific Wallis, Gilbert and Partners sat in this spot. It operated for fifty years until the building was put on the market and a sale was agreed with Trafalgar House, a large UK investment conglomerate.

It's here that the story gets a bit murky. Just before the sale was agreed, an inspector for the Department of the Environment visited the factory and decided to carry out an emergency procedure to list the property as an important building. The idea was to prevent Trafalgar House or future owners altering it without state permission.

Most accounts will agree that Trafalgar House was made aware that the building would soon be protected by law – but as soon as the sale papers were signed, and just before the preservation order could be rubber-stamped, demolition teams were ordered in. Over a three-day weekend, Trafalgar House razed the bulk of the building to the ground.

The public were outraged and, in response, lobby groups and public pressure got a further 150 interwar buildings listed for protection, including the iconic Battersea Power Station.

These days, the remnants of the original factory stand as a cautionary reminder of how easy it is for our built heritage to be destroyed. Whenever I pass these gates, I still feel outrage at how something so beautiful was taken away from our generation – and pride that people fought back to protect other buildings in this book.

COTY COSMETICS FACTORY

Just a little way along from the remains of the Firestone Factory, and on the opposite side of the road, is the old Coty Cosmetics Factory, which was completed in 1932 and designed by – you guessed it – Wallis, Gilbert and Partners.

The working environment all along the Golden Mile was fun back in the 1930s, with most of the employers laying on lavish Christmas parties as well as family picnics and works outings to the coast in the summer. But it didn't stop there: between all the jollies, the staff often took part in inter-factory competitions in all manner of sporting events. Cricket and football matches were fairly common, but so was boxing, would you believe?

The old Coty Factory is the only one along the Golden Mile that's currently lit up at night, and it looks absolutely marvellous.

NATIONAL PROVINCIAL BANK

This rather impressive brick building was built in 1935 and designed by the architect W. F. C. Holden (no relation to Charles Holden of London Underground fame in case you are wondering). It operated as the area's main bank for many years and is situated near the western end of this stretch of road, designed to mirror the look of the neighbouring Gillette Factory.

Holden was a very interesting character. He was a practising artist before and after the First World War and exhibited at the Royal Academy a number of times. During the war he served in the camouflage unit of the Royal Engineers and rose to the rank of captain. He was also awarded the Military Cross in 1918 for gallantry during active operations and designed the British 'camouflage trees' for the War Department, which were fake bomb-damaged hollow trees, made from metal, that were positioned on the Western Front and which an observer could climb into and spy on the enemy from. Some of his war paintings are in the Imperial War Museum collection, as are the original designs for the trees.

After the First World War, he worked as chief architect for the National Provincial Bank and designed a number of buildings, including this one. He even put a proposal together to encase Tower Bridge in glass to reduce the number of times it had to be repainted, an idea rejected as 'ludicrously dangerous'.

He sounds like the sort of chap who deserves a book about his life, but for now we have his wonderful buildings and art.

THE GILLETTE FACTORY

The grand finale of our tour down the Great West Road has got to be the Gillette Factory, sitting on the appropriately named Gillette Corner (a coincidence if ever there was one).

On 6 January 1937, the factory was opened by the Lord Mayor of London, who had the very important job of depressing a button to start the machines. He was followed by the chairman of the company, who also did a good job of depressing things by giving a long, statistics-laden speech on how Gillette helped men with the arduous task of shaving every day. The press lapped up the news that 50,000 miles of facial hair grew in Great Britain each day and this figure appeared in every newspaper in the morning. I'm guessing it was a very, very quiet news day.

The factory was one of the last to be completed on the Great West Road before the onset of war, and by this time the area itself was well and truly established. Indeed, Lord Greenwood, one of the guest speakers at the opening ceremony, described it as 'the golden road of the National Government', with the Gillette Factory being the 'steel milestone of it'.

Gillette left the site in 2006 and since then it's looked empty and disused, but how times have changed since the 1980s when the Firestone Factory was razed to the ground (see page 56). No one would dare drive a bulldozer near it and the site is currently being used as a film studio, with plans to restore and expand it in the works. It seems a valuable lesson was learned on the Golden Mile, and it's heartening to see how much care and expense has gone into preserving our 1930s heritage. Long may it continue.

THE OVALTINE FACTORY
Kings Langley, WD4 8GY

What could be more British than a delicious mug of warm Ovaltine? Well, almost anything really because it turns out that Ovaltine originated in Switzerland.

It was, however, a very popular drink in the UK, particularly in the twentieth century, so much so that a manufacturing plant was set up in Kings Langley, Hertfordshire, in 1913. You'll have to forgive me: this slightly-out-of-the-suburbs factory is so gorgeous that I've included it as an honorary London suburbanite.

The Ovaltine Factory expanded rapidly in the 1920s into what you have in this photo: a stunning early art deco building tucked away in what was then lush countryside. But why Kings Langley and not somewhere a little more populated and with a good road network? Well, to make a lot of Ovaltine it turns out that you need a very large amount of barley, milk and eggs – as well as coal to power the whole enterprise. So, a site was chosen next to the Grand Union Canal, allowing coal

to be brought down from the Midlands, and land around the factory was purchased to establish dedicated dairy, poultry and arable farms.

The factory closed in 2002 and all that is now left is the splendid facade that you can see in these pictures, behind which sit new apartments. Ovaltine is still made, and you can still buy it in Britain, although for most Brits it's probably now just a distant, warm recollection from our childhoods of when we visited Granny's house. The taste lives on in our memories, along with the Ovaltine song 'Because we all drink Ovaltine, we're happy boys and girls'.

THE ADDIS FACTORY
Hertford, SG13 7HH

In 1770, a chap called William Addis was jailed for causing a riot in the Spitalfields area of London. With all that spare time on his hands, he decided to figure out a better way of cleaning teeth. Using an animal bone, glue and some bristles, he invented the toothbrush.

After his release he started manufacturing the design and became very wealthy, eventually passing his new company on to his eldest son. Toothbrushes, however, were still a niche product and it wasn't until the First World War that Addis toothbrushes were used widely, when they were included in soldiers' supply packs. After the war, business boomed, and so these new streamline moderne buildings were constructed about ten miles from the Greater London borders.

If the name Addis sounds vaguely familiar to you, check your washing-up bowl, dustpan and brush or kitchen bin. Addis branched out into homewares in the twentieth century, and they have a habit of sneaking into British homes undetected in the same way as packets of IKEA tea lights do!

THE HOOVER FACTORY
Perivale, UB6 8DF

This former factory is one of the true superstars of London's suburbia, much loved by Londoners and admired by travellers up and down the busy Western Avenue, which heads north-west out of London.

The factory was designed in 1933 by Wallis, Gilbert and Partners (remember those guys?). Although most of us would class it as an art deco building, the term itself didn't come into use until much later, and Thomas Wallis himself described it as 'fancy', the prevailing term for this style at the time.

Interestingly, the colours and shapes that you see in the accents are said to be inspired by Inca and Mayan designs rather than the Egyptian ones which became hugely popular in the 1920s after Howard Carter discovered the tomb of Tutankhamen in 1922.

At the time, the design was considered rather old-fashioned by some critics as it borrowed elements from Victorian architecture (such as the columns). But it became a favourite among locals and the press, who gushed about the place as it started to take shape among the fields of Perivale, with the *Daily Herald* calling it 'more like a child's fairy palace than a factory'.

The factory went on to employ 1,600 people at its peak and became one of the new breed of workplaces that recognised that staff welfare and happiness led to increased productivity.

Production of vacuum cleaners continued at the factory for almost fifty years, and the factory was listed for protection at Grade II*, just before Hoover left in 1982. The listing describes the building as 'possibly the most significant arterial factory of its date, and one of the most attractive'.

After the site was vacated, the building lay empty for nearly ten years until the supermarket chain Tesco bought and refurbished it to create a store out back and office space in the main frontage, opening in the early 1990s. Twenty-five years later, in 2015, the property firm IDM purchased the site, and the main building was converted into luxury apartments, retaining the supermarket in the rear.

BUILDING NUMBER 7
Perivale, UB6 8DW

This building sits right next to the Hoover Factory and it's easy to miss if you're gawping at its big, fancy, show-off neighbour as you zoom along the A40, which is a bit of a shame as if it was sitting next to any other regular building it would be a showstopper. I reckon it could even hold its own in South Beach, Miami, but as it is, it's not even the fanciest building in Perivale.

Building Number 7 was the staff canteen for the Hoover Factory and, if it isn't obvious, it was designed by the same architects as the main factory itself.

So here it is, without its big brother. I mean, the streamlined way that the windows on those two front towers curve around sharply to meet that main tower in the middle is incredible. It's reminiscent of an ocean liner's bow, or maybe even a streamlined railway locomotive. Those side towers remind me of 1930s air-traffic control towers, and just look at all that glass in those amazing window frames!

THE NESTLÉ FACTORY
Hayes, UB3 4QF

In 1889, the winner of a strongman competition in London was a German chap called Eugen Sandow. Sandow, who many believe to be the father of body-building, credited the source of his great strength to chocolate and created 'Sandow's Health & Strength Cocoa'. The production was based in London, and when the business was successful enough to start expanding, he began constructing the early part of this now ex-chocolate factory in Hayes in 1914.

However, 1914 wasn't a good year to be a German in England and he soon found his brand-new factory confiscated and turned over to the government for the production of munitions.

During the war, Sandow's business was sold to another chocolate maker, and in 1919 the site reopened as the Hayes Chocolate Factory. The factory soon needed to expand, and new buildings were designed by Wallis, Gilbert and Partners, which can be seen on the left-hand side of this photo.

The Hayes Cocoa Company lasted about ten years before being bought by the Swiss giants Nestlé, in 1929. Research at the site later resulted in the world's first instant coffee: Nescafé.

Sales of instant coffee took off in the Second World War when it was included in ration packs, and business boomed. Soon after the war, Nestlé moved its UK headquarters to the site and expansion started once more. By the 1990s the factory's main product was coffee and eventually the crumbling site was closed. These days the factory is part of Hayes Village, a large complex of new homes with the original facades restored as you see them now.

But what happened to the German chap, you may ask? Well, if you were to win the Mr Olympia bodybuilding title today (you might), the statuette you'd receive is called the Sandow Trophy, named after Eugen.

THE FRAME FOODS FACTORY
Southfields, SW18 5TF

Nourish & Flourish: wise words indeed, splashed across the front of this unique place in Southfields. This isn't the sort of building one simply drives past on the way to the shops; it's tucked away down a side street between Wandsworth and Wimbledon and is well worth a detour.

The Frame Foods Factory was built in 1903 and there really isn't anything else like it in London. It's covered in bright green faïence tiles with ceramic motifs inset all along its length, reminiscent of the Arts and Crafts style – the highly decorative arts movement of the time, popularised by people like William Morris, John Ruskin and Charles Rennie Mackintosh. It looks amazing in the sun – all shiny and happy.

Frame Foods made its name in the late nineteenth century selling baby food that 'cured rickets and scurvy'. What the baby food was actually made of seemed to be the by-products of flour milling and beer brewing, boiled with gelatine into some kind of lumpy jelly. If you can imagine slimy porridge with Marmite in it, you wouldn't be far off. Anyhow, the mums of the day glowed about it in Frame's adverts, with one proclaiming that it 'straightened Phyllis's legs out wonderfully'. Phyllis, I imagine, was just relieved that she no longer needed to be force-fed lumpy Marmite slime any more.

For some unknown reason, Frame Foods vanished about the time that the sun was discovered to cure rickets, and today the building is made up of apartments.

THE OLD VINYL FACTORY
Hayes, UB3 1HA

The Old Vinyl Factory is part of a complex of industrial buildings in Hayes and is absolutely massive – at its peak it covered 150 acres and employed 22,000 local people.

The first building went up in 1907 and belonged to the Gramophone and Typewriter Company, which made, well, gramophones and typewriters. During the First World War, the factory was commandeered to make armaments, but as soon as the war was over the business took off again.

By 1927, new buildings were needed to keep up with demand, so Wallis, Gilbert and Partners (yes, them again) were employed to design huge new factories and depositories, including the one you see here.

The site continued expanding as the business merged with other companies, and by the 1960s, as teenagers spent their cash on records by the likes of The Beatles and Cliff Richard, Hayes record production was at its peak. Sadly, the introduction of the cassette tape in the 1970s led to the decline of vinyl production, and by 1996 the factories were abandoned.

In 2011, the site was bought by developers, and since then it's been construction galore, with hundreds of flats and light-industrial units going up in both the old and newly constructed buildings. There's now a mix of almost every architectural style from the last 120 years on those 150 acres, and I must say, it's pretty incredible to see it all. There's even a small vinyl pressing factory on the site again. How cool is that?

GLOBE CENTRAL
Twickenham, TW1 1LX

If you've ever been stuck in a traffic jam near Twickenham Rugby Stadium, you'll know this one!

Today, Globe Central is an apartment building, but before that it was an industrial unit, and before *that* it was a factory.

It's always looked recognisably 1930s, but since it's been converted to flats it's been given the full art deco treatment, with a fresh lick of pastel paint and a splash of 1950s chrome installed.

Others might disagree, but I think it's refreshing to see how well the building has been restored. I remember the state of most art deco buildings in the 1980s, rotting and grimy, on the verge of being demolished. It might not have the lived-in charm of other old buildings any more, but the love and care that buildings like this, the Ovaltine Factory, the Pyrene Factory and even the Hoover Factory have received mean that we can continue to appreciate the architecture in the present day. And that's something very special, isn't it?

THE DE HAVILLAND STUDIOS
Hackney, E5 9NY

Don't be fooled, all you aviation buffs: this building has nothing to do with the aircraft manufacturer de Havilland! Disappointing, I know.

This beautifully modernist building was a canning factory built in the 1930s, and its biggest claim to fame is that it was designed by Sir Owen Williams. Who's that? Why, only the same chap who designed the original Wembley Stadium, the Dorchester Hotel and the Empire Pool. Some say he's one of the great pioneers of British modernism! Pretty cool for a small factory down a side road in Hackney, right?

THE DE HAVILLAND FACTORY SITE
Hertfordshire, AL10 9SJ

And in comparison, here's the real de Havilland airfield and aircraft factory. It fell out of use in 1993 and sits about seven miles outside the M25 in the town of Hatfield in Hertfordshire. Remember the Comet Hotel we saw earlier (see page 40)? Well, it's about a ten-minute walk away from this site, and one of the first aircraft built here, in 1934, was that little red DH88 Comet they've got a model of.

The de Havilland company itself was one of the pioneers of aviation in the UK and was building aircraft well before the First World War on its earlier site in Edgware. Business was good, and by the 1930s they needed a bigger site so moved out here to an enormous campus of factories, offices and, of course, an aerodrome.

These days you can still see a lot of the original buildings. They have been re-purposed, naturally, but to take a look it's a simple matter of parking and having a wander – and as an added bonus, if a few hundred yards of walking has made you hungry, you can pop into one of them and pick up a KFC Bargain Bucket (or wander down to the Comet Hotel for a cocktail if you're thirsty). In fact, all three of the buildings on this site featured in this book are within a couple of hundred yards of each other.

The main administration building of the complex, which you see on the right, was opened in 1934 and now serves as Hatfield Police Station and Magistrates Court. It's fair to say that, like a lot of old buildings, it could do with a lick of paint. Let's hope that once all the local villains have been caught and locked up, the police officers will have a bit more time on their hands to get round to it.

On the right you'll see a neat little building that used to be one of the site's gatehouses. It's now the offices of a company that finds accommodation for students, and sits between the old canteen block (there it is, in the background) and our next building, which was not a canteen block but sort of is now.

I reckon this is one of the coolest-looking KFCs in the world. It was built in 1934 and was the home of de Havilland's personnel department. Back then, you might have gone in there to pick up your weekly wage – which averaged about £2.50. These days, if you took £2.50 into this building, you'd be able to walk out the proud owner of a small bag of fries.

THE CARRERAS FACTORY
Camden, NW1 7AW

This magnificent building was originally the Carreras Tobacco Factory. It was designed in an Egyptian art deco style, which was all the rage in the 1920s after Tutankhamun's tomb was discovered in 1922.

Known at the time for producing the highly popular Craven A cigarettes – the packets of which featured a black cat – the Carreras Factory itself featured many black cats. So many, in fact, that most Londoners refer to the building as the Black Cat Factory.

To this day, the building looks incredibly striking – but one can only imagine what it must have been like when it opened in 1928. On its official opening day, the pavement outside was covered in sand, actors in Egyptian costume were brought in, and chariot races were held on the road in front. The 1920s were brilliant! I'd love to see someone try that in the 2020s if they opened a factory in London. We'd just walk by, soya latte in hand, and try to pretend it wasn't happening.

PART 2

THE GREAT EXPANSION

FROM HOUSES TO HOMES

With all the new roads, railways, factories and offices springing up outside of the inner city, millions of Londoners began to move further out. At first, houses were built by local authorities, but following the Chamberlain Housing Act of 1923, subsidies came into the hands of the private sector. Big developers such as Wates, Wimpey, Laing and Davis Estates produced conservative designs that sold well; designs that were reminiscent of the England of old, Tudor and Elizabethan cottages, arranged in rows.

Then, in 1934, the *Daily Mail*'s annual Ideal Home Exhibition tried to shake things up. Traditionally, the Ideal Home Exhibition was a place where house builders, home furnishers and gadget manufacturers showed and sold their wares. But in that year, the show decided to encourage mainstream house builders of the day to construct more futuristic homes. So, in the National Hall of Olympia, the exhibition displayed several full-sized show homes: flat-roofed modernist houses with all the latest mod cons built into the fabric of the house. Prospective purchasers were encouraged to place orders for these homes, which would then be built in the new suburbs.

Unfortunately, most people didn't trust the combination of the British weather and a flat roof (which were notorious for leaks), so only a handful of the Ideal Home Exhibition houses were ever sold and built in the real world, along with a few other speculative designs from developers and architects. They were nearly all built in 1935 and are true gems within London's suburbs.

A VERY SPECIAL HOUSE
Stoneleigh, Surrey

Where else to begin but with a house that's very special to me – and partly why this book exists?

I grew up on a 1930s suburban housing estate in northern Surrey. Every six months, my mum and I would drive to the dentist's several miles away, and on every trip we'd pass this house. With its clean lines and black-and-white blocky facade, it stood out from all the other homes in the area. I thought it was incredible. I was never really the sort of kid who wanted to fit in, but I was always being told that I should; this house showed me that it was okay to just be myself.

Fast-forward many years, and I found myself living back in suburbia. When I started my Instagram account, I remembered this house and went looking for it. My search took me to countless other homes, and I slowly and surely fell back in love with art deco (as you might have noticed), but I couldn't find this one anywhere.

As the months passed by, I had just about given up looking for it, thinking the house must have been a romantic childhood memory, when I got a message from a very nice chap recommending I see a house in Stoneleigh. I knew straight away which house it must be and slightly lost my cool.

To me, this house represents nostalgia for my childhood, uncompromising beauty, and some important life decisions that I've made. A beautiful old building is often more than just a pile of bricks; it's sometimes a page marker in our personal story.

And as a little bonus, it turned out that there were four of these houses, all sitting next to each other in the same street, and not just the one that I remembered.

SUNSPAN HOUSE
New Malden, Royal Borough of Kingston upon Thames

Sunspan houses were one of the designs showcased at the 1934 Ideal Home Exhibition at Olympia. Designed by Wells Coates, they were marketed as 'the home of the future', and the idea was to let as much sun into the home as possible. Instead of the front elevation facing the road, with the rear in the garden, the building was built in a diamond shape. This simple but radical idea meant that the rear corner of the building always faced due south and featured wrap-around sun windows that let the light in from dawn to dusk. About fifteen were eventually built, and of the ten or so that I've seen, all are aligned in this way, with a south-facing garden.

This lovely house is in New Malden in the southern suburbs and is owned by Andy and Sharon, who have recently moved in. They are renovating the house fabulously, using modern materials to restore it to its 1930s heyday. It really is an astonishing property and was originally bought by a Jewish family; until recently, it had a mezuzah on the doorpost right next to that amazing curved front door.

It's a shame that only a dozen or so of these houses still exist, as simply turning the house a quarter of a turn is such a great idea. Thankfully, all the ones I've seen are in exquisite condition and don't look like they are going anywhere soon.

It's interesting to note that these houses are generally built in groups of three, and all but two are within a mile of the old London-to-Portsmouth Road.

HOUSE NO. 9
West Wickham, London Borough of Bromley

Another lovely building originally showcased in the National Hall of the Ideal Home Exhibition in 1934 was simply named 'House No. 9'. It was offered for sale or order by Morrell (Builders) Ltd and was designed by the architects Leslie H. Kemp and Frederick E. Tasker.

These houses featured maplewood flooring throughout, and glazed double doors separating the rooms on the ground floor could be opened to make one single room that was forty foot long, 'an excellent feature when holding an impromptu dance', a brochure claimed.

Besides all the usual mod cons of the day, like a fitted kitchen and hot and cold running water, wiring points were added to the walls to allow the connection of electric clocks or loudspeakers. A single wireless receiving set could be operated by remote control and was situated in a telephone booth, which I believe was under the stairs.

The design was also offered in red brick with a pitched roof, which seems a terrible shame, but as far as I know only two of the modernist version featured here were built in London. Thankfully, both are listed for protection – at the time of writing, this building is being used as a temporary library while its twin in Brixton has just been handsomely restored.

A HOME WITH A HISTORY
Purley, London Borough of Croydon

This wonderful home was surely one of the inspirations for the houses exhibited at the Ideal Home Exhibition, as it predates the show by eight years and is one of the first examples of a modernist house in the UK. It was built in 1926 by George Cushing, a surveyor from Croydon, only one year after what we now tend to call 'art deco' was showcased to the world as 'style moderne' at the Exposition Internationale des Arts Décoratifs et Industriels Modernes in Paris – a huge exhibition, sponsored by the French government, that presented the most up-to-date styles from around the world. Until this exposition, this type of design was almost exclusively found only in France and Belgium.

Almost a hundred years later, this house is still perched high on a very steep hill and in immaculate condition, having been extensively renovated by its current owners, Paul and Jenny, who spent eighteen months stripping the house back to its bare skeleton and rebuilding using modern materials while maintaining its 1920s character.

Some of the features that they found during the renovation are a testament to its original owners and the way they lived. The home initially included quarters for a maid (and an electric bell in the sitting room with which to summon her), and a levelled garden built into the very steep hill, where legendary tennis parties were held. Since the renovation, Paul and Jenny have been carefully selecting their beautiful fixtures and fittings, ranging from an art nouveau fireguard to a mid-century sideboard.

And for those of you wondering who those first owners were – they're more familiar than you'd think! The original owner and builder, George Cushing, was the father of Peter Cushing, an actor most famous for his roles in the

Hammer House of Horror films of the 1950s to 1970s in which he played Baron von Frankenstein and Dr Van Helsing. He also played the commander of the Death Star, Grand Moff Tarkin, in *Star Wars*. A much-loved and gentlemanly professional by all accounts, who became a legend in his own lifetime: there's a blue plaque on the house to celebrate the great man himself.

This house is far more than it seems at first glance: not only is it as stunning on the inside as it is on the outside, but it also holds a special place in popular culture. The force is strong in this one.

A FAMILY HOME

Worcester Park, Royal Borough of Kingston upon Thames

Behind each of these fine houses are – of course – the people who have made them their homes.

This appealing house sits just around the corner from Malden Manor Station in South-West London, and is believed to have been designed by Barnes-based architect L. Norman Holt in 1935. It's currently owned by two sisters, Luciana and Silvana, and is special to them as it was their childhood home. It has been in their family for over fifty years, having been bought in 1972 – in fact, Mum and Dad fell in love with the house so much they put in an offer without even viewing the inside.

Little of this place has changed since then; it's a real time capsule. To give you an idea, all the original inner walls are in place, there is different dark wood flooring on each of the three floors, and it even has all its original doors, incredible tiled bathrooms and a tiny 1930s garage.

The sisters' parents sadly passed away about a year before I met them and they dread having to sell the house. Although they are willing to sell, the home has meant so much to their family that they don't want it to be sold to someone who doesn't appreciate it and are scared a property developer might knock it down. Sometimes buildings are more important to us than we realise – and I'm proud to have had the honour of capturing this house as a reminder of the happy years Luciana and Silvana's family spent there.

THE HOUSE IN THE WOODS
Loughton, Essex

At the beginning of 1937, the road that this house is now sitting on was partially completed. It led to a clearing in Epping Forest and a popular local pub, and was a particularly idyllic spot, overlooking that clearing and the Monk Wood part of the forest. When plots of land were being sold, soon-to-be-married Florence Brookes seized the opportunity and bought Plot 3, with plans to build a stunning modernist home with her new husband. By 1939, the house was complete, and what a house it was, contrasting with the rural environment delightfully.

With the huge growth of London, this area is now well and truly part of the outer London suburbs, but Epping Forest remains a massive oasis of trees in among all those family homes. Because of the protected status of the forest, the road around this house was only developed on one side, so it still overlooks a clearing in the woods.

The house has a really simple design, essentially a box with a rounded-off corner, but unlike most boxy houses the windows curve round that corner, letting in oodles of light. It's still got its original garage, which is pretty rare today, and there's also a feature that you see surprisingly often in houses like this: a first-floor door leading to a tiny balcony with no railings. What on earth were they thinking?

SUNSHINE HOUSE
Chingford, London Borough of Waltham Forest

This sunny house, perched high on a hill, was built in 1939 and originally owned by Frank Miller, an eccentric pharmacist well known for boring a hole in the ceiling of his pharmacy so that he could install a home-made conveyer belt that delivered medicines to customers waiting in awe. He made a number of adaptations to his own house too: one of the large windows was hinged at the bottom via a broomstick axle and could open to ninety degrees using an electric motor; he cladded the inside of the house in Formica and polystyrene tiles; he built a clock into the living-room ceiling; and, as he had used the wiring from inside an electric blanket to wrap round the water pipes to stop them freezing in the winter, he also installed a light on a wall that came on to let you know that the water pipes were electrically charged!

By the time the house was bought by its second owner, Howard, in 1983, it was in a terrible state. The fabric of the house was crumbling and all the home-made gadgets and plastic cladding had put potential buyers off. Howard, who still lives there, picked it up for £20,000 less than the neighbouring house had gone for, and set about repairing it.

As the plastic came off the walls and ceilings, the long-hidden art deco features of the house started to become apparent. Back in the 1980s, art deco was not particularly fashionable, but Howard rather liked it and so began a forty-year journey of restoring the place to its former glory. He's done an amazing job, and the house is full of original features and 1930s collectables.

And if you're wondering about that incredible front door, Howard had that made in the 1980s because he thought most people's front doors were boring. The house is an absolute marvel and testament to two unique and very different owners, who made their own rules. True suburban heroes, as far as I'm concerned.

CUBIST PLAYGROUND
Twickenham, London Borough of Richmond upon Thames

This beautiful cubist-influenced house near Twickenham has recently undergone an extensive renovation and it's such an impressive house it just had to make an appearance. It was designed by Couch & Coupland in 1935, who were well known at the time for designing large blocks of flats in outer London. It is currently owned by Marcus, an author, public speaker and force of nature, who inherited the house from his much-loved parents after they passed away in 2018.

Marcus is as much a suburban gem as the house, and while he lives in the property, he also gives public-speaking lessons there, as well as opening its doors to authors, librarians and educators with the aim of promoting literacy. What's more, since he's moved back in, Marcus has renovated the place, removing the rotten wooden structure of the home and installing a huge sprung dance floor, a library, a teaching bunker in the garden and even a zip wire in the back.

Marcus and his house really sum up suburbia for me: you might know what to expect of a particular area, but turn the corner and there's a house like this waiting for you with an extraordinary person living inside.

Looking up: an ultra-modern concrete spiral staircase

MODERNIST COTTAGE
Northwood Hills, London Borough of Hillingdon

This lovely house in the north-west suburbs is one of a group of four similar houses, each with a different-coloured set of roof tiles. The little enclave was described in Nikolaus Pevsner's 1951 *Buildings of England* series as 'a few half-hearted efforts at a flat-roofed modern style', but I must admit that these are some of my favourite houses in the suburbs. I love the fact that although it must have been a radical modern design back in 1934, it still feels like a cosy cottage, which is quite a clever trick to pull off when you think about it.

When I went to visit the site, I met Julia and Adrian, who own this property and have lived here for over a decade. As you can imagine, they love their house and have put a lot of effort into preserving it, including cool features such as the original banisters, Bakelite door handles and the 1930s metal-framed Crittall windows.

A MODERNIST'S DREAM
Woking, Surrey

You don't see many 1930s modernist mansions like this in suburbia, but they are around, usually tucked away in gated communities or hiding behind huge hedges. When you do spot one in the flesh, they are breathtaking! This particular house certainly fits the definition of a mansion and sits in woodland, hidden behind a big hedge and overlooking a golf course – though you can easily see the house through its enormous and fancy gates from the busy A245 just outside Woking.

Over the years the house has been greatly extended by its subsequent owners. It started life as the box-shaped building that you can see in the centre, and since then a glass-fronted garage and large recreational building in the garden have been added, among other things.

I always think of this house as the front gates on the way out of suburbia to Surrey, and love that even with all the changes made, this beautiful home has kept true to the modernist ideals it started out with and is bang up to date, stylish and comfortable.

FLATS: GOING UP IN THE WORLD

As well as thousands of new houses going up all over the countryside, a new type of suburban building was starting to appear in the 1920s: flats.

In Central London, apartment blocks were nothing new. Since the 1880s, wealthy Londoners had used apartments as a base during the social season, when they flocked to the inner city, abandoning the comfort of their country homes. These large, early mansion blocks can still be seen in areas like Kensington and Regent's Park and were built with accommodation for a small cohort of servants.

Things changed when local authorities were given subsidies to build social housing through the 1919 Addison Act. It was at about this time that the term 'flats' was first coined, as councils set about building small garden estates and low-rise blocks of about five storeys.

When the Chamberlain Housing Act came along in 1923, a lot of these subsidies shifted to the private sector, and developers joined in the flat-building frenzy. Blocks of flats sprang up all over the suburbs, often in the more built-up areas where space was at a premium, and they came in all shapes and sizes, from a single block of eight through to vast estates.

Because flat building was a fairly new concept back then and there was no set formula as to what to include in the design, today we are left with an amazing and diverse legacy of interwar apartment buildings with sometimes bewildering features.

OAKLANDS ESTATE
Clapham, SW4 8NH

I have to admit that this is quite a deceptive photo as the building that this is part of is huge – the whole estate covers three acres – but I couldn't resist sharing a close-up of those windows and lovely balconies.

Built in 1936 by the London County Council, Oaklands Estate was constructed as part of the Labour Party's policy to relieve overcrowding in the city. Living conditions for working-class families were so dire that increasing social housing was a Labour Party priority – to the point that 'Up with the houses and down with the slums' was the slogan of the day.

New council tenants at Oaklands Estate were treated to a number of modern innovations, including a built-in larder, a kitchenette, a copper hot-water tank, and a communal clothes-drying room on the top floor. The building featured in the *Architects Journal* and, incredibly, the total cost for the project was £87,970, which is about the same price as a single garage in Clapham today. (I kid you not!).

THE GRAMPIANS
Shepherds Bush, W6 7LN

If you've ever been stuck in traffic between Shepherds Bush and Hammersmith, you probably know this building well: it's one of those places that you can't help staring at.

The design for the Grampians was first exhibited at the Royal Academy in 1935 by architect Maurice Webb, who also designed the guildhall and Bentalls department store in Kingston. Architecture clearly ran in the family: Maurice's father, Sir Aston Webb, designed Buckingham Palace (well, the east facade of the palace, at least) as well as Admiralty Arch on the Mall.

I was told by a lovely resident that the Grampians was named after the Scottish mountain range, as it was intended to tower over the local environment and bring beauty and grandeur to the area. I'm not sure how true that is – and personally I wonder if this massive building was Maurice's way of coping with an inferiority complex. If it was, I hope his dad was suitably impressed!

DU CANE COURT
Balham, SW17 7JA

Built between 1935 and 1938, Du Cane Court was once considered a luxury mansion block and came equipped with a restaurant, a private club with a snooker table, a cards room, a roof terrace, its own shop and postal service and two bars.

The block is so big that it has different postcodes. Rumour has it that these postcodes affect home insurance premiums, with one end of the block reportedly having markedly cheaper insurance than the other.

ROSEHILL COURT
Sutton, SM4 6JT

These remarkable flats sit above several shops on a busy and very big roundabout, and incredibly for this day and age, there's almost no information available on them. Although thousands of people drive past them every day, they are easy to miss, as generally people are more concerned with not hitting the cars around them than looking up. Actually, that's probably a good thing, isn't it?

KINGSLEY COURT
Willesden Green, NW2 5TJ

This pleasing building was designed in 1935 by Peter Caspari, who started his professional career in Berlin. Caspari was Jewish and in the early 1930s worked on projects with Albert Speer, who later went on to become the Third Reich's principal architect. By 1933 it was clear that Germany was becoming a dangerous place for Caspari, especially as he had been involved in anti-Nazi demonstrations, and he fled to England via Switzerland to escape imminent arrest.

Once in the UK he found work with Davis Estates, a prolific building company specialising in suburban homes, and designed the building we have here in North-West London. By 1936 Caspari had set up his own practice and went on to design about a dozen mansion blocks in suburbia before moving to Toronto and becoming one of Canada's foremost architects. Peter Caspari is someone I had never heard of before I started exploring suburbia, but he's become a real hero of mine, with an incredible life and a wonderful legacy.

HIGHTREES HOUSE
Clapham, SW12 8AH

Hightrees House is a handsome art deco mansion block which overlooks Clapham Common. It was designed by R. W. H. Jones, who is also the architect responsible for Saltdean Lido, a gorgeous modernist outdoor pool on the south coast.

Interestingly, if you're a UK lawyer, the name 'Hightrees House' might ring a bell. This is because the building features in a textbook legal case about 'promissory estoppel' (nope, me neither). When the building opened in 1938, with the war on the horizon, hardly anyone wanted to move in, so the few existing residents negotiated a 50 per cent reduction in ground rent. This was great for the residents – except that after the war ended, the landlords not only put the ground rent back up but tried to charge back rent for six years. The landlords thought that they were entitled to get their money back as no legally binding contract had been signed; they had only sent a letter to the tenants detailing the rent reduction. So the landlords and the tenants went to court to determine if a letter of promise could be considered a legally binding contract. The tenants won and English legal precedent was set. (My apologies to all lawyers reading this: I know it's more complicated than that, but this is a book about the suburbs, not about laws with funny-sounding Latin names.)

CAPEL GARDENS & PINNER COURT
Pinner, HA5 5RG

In charmingly suburban Pinner, there are two glamorous 1930s blocks of flats built in the hacienda style: with brightly coloured roofs, superb windows, balconies with elaborate iron railings, and plenty of arches. We don't really associate haciendas with the London suburbs – in fact, they're pretty rare in the UK – but these flats were built with the aim of bringing a bit of Hollywood glamour to the 'burbs.

From the conversations I've had with the current residents, it seems that they love living there; but keeping those original windows in top condition is a labour of love, and in the cold British winters it's not uncommon to find ice on the inside of them. It seems that you can bring Hollywood style to the London suburbs, but not the weather.

CHOLMELEY LODGE
Highgate, N6 5EN

Cholmeley Lodge was built in 1934 and is said to be the inspiration for Florin Court in Clerkenwell (see page 148) – the building used as Hercule Poirot's home in the beloved TV series.

This block was originally proposed for Bournemouth, but the local planning committee felt it was too out-there for the seaside town and demanded that Tudor-style timberwork be added. The architect basically said 'bollocks to that' and built it in Highgate instead. The flats are now Grade II listed.

FLORIN COURT
Barbican, EC1M 6EU

Florin Court (or Whitehaven Mansions to all the Agatha Christie fans out there) is most definitely not in the suburbs, as it sits bang in the middle of London, but as it was the home and office of Hercule Poirot in the classic 1990s TV series, I thought I should make an exception and include it. It's a glorious building, with specially made beige bricks and sweeping streamline moderne curves. Back when it was built in 1936, the ground floor had a porter's office and flat to accommodate him at night, as well as marble flooring. In the basement there was a public restaurant, a cocktail bar and a club room. And, as if that's not enough, there was also an indoor swimming pool, a sauna, a gym, a lounge, a library, a laundry room, a parking garage, a huge roof terrace overlooking the city and a separate building containing two squash courts. It's one of those places where if you have to ask how much it costs to live there, you probably can't afford to.

SUBURBAN INSTITUTIONS

As suburbia expanded, with ever more housing estates, new infrastructure was put in place to support all these new suburbanites. Doctors' surgeries, hospitals, police stations, schools, libraries and civic buildings (such as Walthamstow Assembly Hall on the left) were built all over the outskirts of London, as well as commercial infrastructure such as power stations, pumping stations and electrical substations.

Very early on, these corporations had figured out that it would be expensive to build in traditional but ornate styles that had been in vogue up until then, so new modernist designs with simple lines and almost no ornamentation became the way forward. Some organisations went all-in on the minimalist approach, building little more than brick boxes with windows, while others created some really out-there designs. This often resulted in strongly worded letters to the local papers from people with far too much time on their hands.

New churches and other places of worship made an appearance too, although, as many of the suburbs were built around villages with their own existing churches, there aren't a huge number of these. Given the more conservative leanings of Christianity back then, finding a modernist church in suburbia is like finding a bishop at a strip club: unexpected yet strangely satisfying.

GREENWICH TOWN HALL
Greenwich, SE10 8RD

London is absolutely peppered with fabulous 1930s civic centres, and Greenwich Town Hall is one of my favourites. This building was designed by Clifford Culpin and inspired by the Dutch architect Willem Dudok, and bears a striking resemblance to Hilversum Town Hall in the Netherlands.

Similar to many other council buildings in London at the time, the new Greenwich Town Hall came about as part of the council's expansion. As more people moved to suburbia, councils took on a greater role and needed more space. They spared no expense when it came to building their new accommodation, leaving us with buildings with some awesome features like this huge clock tower. A local joke at the time was that if you went to see the council, you should probably carry a watch: the councillors were always desperate to know the time as the clocks on each side of the tower showed different times!

ALEXANDRA HOUSE
Brentford, TW8 0JJ

Built in 1938 by Middlesex County Council, this Grade II listed building was originally a health centre and labour exchange. It housed a collection of doctors – rather like a current GP's practice – with some of the additional services you may find at a hospital these days.

If you're wondering what a health centre was like before the NHS, I can tell you that for most people it wasn't a very nice place to visit. If you were employed, the centre wouldn't charge fees for services, but if you were a stay-at-home partner, unemployed or a child, then your care came at a cost. Avoiding paying for medical care until it was absolutely necessary meant the waiting rooms were often crammed with very sick and infectious women, children and the elderly.

After the war ended, we started to look after our most vulnerable more, by putting in place better social security and the NHS. Alexandra House has now been bought by a local primary school, and so a building that was once full of sick and desperate families is today full of happy, laughing primary-school kids, blissfully unaware of our shared past.

LADY BANKES SCHOOL
Ruislip, HA4 9SF

This fantastic example of municipal architecture in Middlesex was erected to serve the new suburb that was being built around it in 1936. Very soon after it first opened, the local schools inspector visited and earnestly informed a group of 150 pupils aged five and upwards that they were now full-time scholars and as such should no longer accept offers of employment! He was being deadly serious and many of the five-year-olds had to give up their high-paying jobs in the City to concentrate on learning their times tables.

WILLIAM TORBITT SCHOOL
Ilford, IG3 7SS

Opened in 1937, it's a miracle that the William Torbitt Primary School is still standing: it was hit and repaired three times during the Second World War, though thankfully there were no casualties. This building is a beautiful reminder to me of how lucky we are to be at peace in the UK.

These two schools offer an interesting architectural contrast, don't they? Curvy streamline moderne influences on the opposite page and angular art deco inspirations on this one.

ST PATRICK'S CHURCH
Barking, IG11 9SQ

This is a Barking mad church, isn't it? If you've ever wondered what kind of church a cinema architect would design (yes, that's right, a cinema architect), you've come to the right place. St Patrick's in Barking was consecrated in 1940 and was designed by cinema architect A. E. Wiseman. The whole building cost £10,500, and I think it's probably my favourite church in the whole of the suburbs. If I had a spare ten grand, I'd definitely get myself one.

DAGENHAM CIVIC CENTRE
Dagenham, RM10 7BN

Designed by prolific town-hall architect Ernest Berry Webber, Dagenham's old town hall is massive, grandiose and, despite being in a very built-up area of the suburbs, surrounded by elegant wide, open green spaces. I'm guessing the councillors applied a completely different set of planning rules when they gave themselves permission to build this.

SHIRLEY LIBRARY
Croydon, CR0 8BH

Now this is an unusual sight in the London suburbs: pastel-coloured art deco looking all jolly and pleased with itself. You could almost imagine that you were in Miami, couldn't you?

This 85-year-old little ray of sunshine was built in 1937 as a temporary library and was extended in 1988.

LEATHERHEAD PUMPING STATION
Surrey, KT22 9DR

This pumping station was built in 1935 and was used to – you guessed it – pump water. Water companies back then were all about flexing their corporate egos and demonstrating how powerful and grand they were, so for a building with a functional purpose, it's incredibly showy!

WALTHAM FOREST TOWN HALL
Walthamstow, E17 4JF

This is the headquarters of the London Borough of Waltham Forest; it's recently undergone a major renovation and looks glorious. Designed by Philip Hepworth, the building was finished at the height of war in 1942,

in a style described as a mix of 'stripped classicism' with Bauhaus influences. Architectural scholars do love sticking things in boxes, but I presume what they mean is that it has classical features like grand columns but they are toned down, leaving a kind of budget Greek temple.

Whatever the style is called, there is no denying that the star of the show is the huge green lighthouse clock sticky-up thing that someone has glued to the roof. It even shows (roughly) the right time.

The renovation, although extremely expensive, has been done to preserve it for future generations. One generation that is very happy about this is our current crop of young kids, who love to run through the new light-up splash fountains. It's a building worth going out of your way to see if you're in London; they even hold illumination events there and a Christmas market.

BATTERSEA POWER STATION
Nine Elms, SW11 8AL

For South Londoners, Battersea Power Station has become an iconic waymarker, an industrial masterpiece that sits near the centre of London and marks the beginning of the end of the morning commute into London by train from the southern suburbs. These days, most wouldn't consider this part of Battersea to be in suburbia, but it certainly was when the power station was built, sitting as it does on the river between the Victorian suburbs of Battersea and Chelsea.

So how did a power station end up being such an iconic landmark? Well, at the time of the proposal there was a lot of local unrest at a huge power station being built in the neighbourhood, so a host of architects and engineers were employed to design a magnificent exterior in the latest style (art deco). It was a way of endearing Londoners to the building and proved popular straight away, becoming an instant London landmark, which it remains to this day. This was probably unsurprising given that one of the lead architects, Sir Giles Gilbert Scott, came from a family of architects who between them had already designed iconic landmarks such as the Midland Grand Hotel at St Pancras, the Albert Memorial and Dulwich College. In his own lifetime, Sir Giles Gilbert Scott would also design the Bankside Power Station (now the Tate Modern) as well as the iconic red telephone box.

It was built in two parts; the first half, Battersea A, is to the right-hand side in the picture and was finished in 1935, located close to the Thames for cooling water and coal deliveries. The second part, Battersea B, is a mirror of the first and was finished in 1955, after being delayed because of the Second World War.

Battersea Power Station served London until 1978, when it was decommissioned. There have been many attempts to re-purpose it over the years, but it sat unused until the mid 2010s, when it was sold to a Malaysian property firm who began to redevelop it. It opened in 2022 as a housing and entertainment venue.

The Grade II* listed power station is now surrounded by multimillion-pound apartments. It's quite a bizarre sight, but constructing the apartments was the only way to finance the refurbishment of the power station.

The iconic chimneys were completely rebuilt in 2016 by hand-pouring 25,000 wheelbarrows full of concrete into reconstructions of the original moulds. It's not clear what happened to all those wheelbarrows; I did check eBay, but I presume they were snapped up before I got there.

PART 3

LIVING THE (SUBURBAN) LIFE

OLD BUILDINGS, NEW USES

As people flocked to the suburbs, enter the entrepreneurs who – sensing a handsome profit to be made – set about building new entertainment venues all over the suburbs. In the post-war boom, shops expanded, ultra-modern car showrooms appeared, new cinemas sprang up on every suburban high street, and speedway tracks and greyhound-racing stadiums popped up out of nowhere. Life was good.

Of course, things change and people change, and a lot of those amazing old venues have since closed and been repurposed as people have gone from going out to staying in and binge-watching reality TV (I plead guilty as charged). Cinemas have become bingo halls and churches, and stadiums have become housing, to meet the needs of locals.

Seeing how those old buildings have been preserved and given a new lease of life is incredible – and I love it when I spot the few that are still doing what their makers intended them to do from the beginning: making people happy by entertaining them.

THE ROUNDHOUSE PUB
Dagenham, RM8 2HY

Built in 1936 as part of the Becontree Estate, this pub in Dagenham sits on the western edge of what was the largest council estate in Europe at the time. It later reinvented itself as a live music venue in 1969, and to say it was East London's premier music venue is not an unfounded boast. Some of the acts that played here include Led Zeppelin, Jethro Tull, Deep Purple, T. Rex, Procol Harum, Free, Derek and the Dominos, Supertramp, The Velvet Underground, Yes, Fleetwood Mac, Pink Floyd, Elton John, Nazareth, Hawkwind, Motörhead, Status Quo, ELO, Genesis, Thin Lizzy, Judas Priest, UFO and Queen!

The very loud party ended in 1975, following some not very surprising complaints from the neighbours about noise (Motörhead, noisy?), and after that, the pub rocked on as an iconic local boozer and is still standing to this day.

RANDALLS OF UXBRIDGE
Uxbridge, UB1 1RS

Randalls was a family-run business that started as a furniture maker's in Wycombe in the late nineteenth century. Some of the Randall family subsequently moved to Uxbridge in the 1880s and opened a store which, by 1900, had the distinction of being the first in the town with electric lights. It was said to be 'the brilliant illumination' of this store that attracted customers and helped the business be a success. Since then, many other shops in the UK have installed electric lights.

The business continued expanding and on 11 May 1939 a new art deco store was opened to the public. The grand opening was a very 1930s affair,

and the main attractions were advertised in the local paper, which no doubt brought the crowds in. The headline event? A carpet-weaving demonstration!

All joking aside, Randalls is a lovely building. The huge storefront windows allowed a view straight into the furniture showroom, an incredible innovation at the time. The architect, William Eves, went on to join the architect's office at the nearby council and was awarded an MBE in the 1939 honours list. Of course, like most independent department stores, Randalls was a casualty of online shopping. Fortunately, unlike most, the building has been saved and turned into apartments which boast a very chic art deco frontage indeed.

WALTHAMSTOW GREYHOUND STADIUM

Walthamstow, E4 8SJ

It's hard to believe today, but once upon a time, greyhound racing was a huge sport in Britain. Between the wars, there were thirty-three greyhound stadiums in London alone, and news outlets of the day even called it the UK's national sport.

Back then, a night at the dogs was not a fancy affair like horse racing was; it was very much a male working-class sport and was all about placing bets, with huge amounts of money changing hands among the throngs of flat-capped geezers. The stadiums themselves were often built as multi-use venues, and when the sprightly canines weren't belting round the track pursuing toy rabbits, the arenas held events as diverse as athletics, speedway, and stock-car and banger racing.

Walthamstow Stadium opened in 1929, with the art deco entranceway opening in 1933. It was one of London's premier dog-racing stadiums, with its annual turnover peaking in 1946 at seven million pounds (about a quarter of a billion pounds in today's money!). But attitudes change and by the turn of the twenty-first century, people just weren't going to the dogs any more, leaving the old stadiums empty and crumbling. Walthamstow hung on until 2008, when it was eventually redeveloped as housing, leaving only the frontage, the old tote board and a few smaller buildings as a reminder of very different times.

HIGHBURY STADIUM
Highbury, N5 1EY

Hardcore football fans will find this building very familiar: it's the former home of Arsenal. Designed by prolific football-ground architect Archibald Leitch, the pitch is now a communal garden and part of the Highbury Square development of 711 properties.

Fun fact: the nearest Tube station was originally called Gillespie Road; it was renamed Arsenal in 1932, and is the only Underground station named after a football club.

QUEEN ELIZABETH STADIUM
Enfield, EN1 3PL

This is the home of Enfield Town FC and a hub for local athletics where many successful British athletes have trained, including Olympic gold medallists Sebastian Coe, Daley Thompson and Linford Christie. The stadium sits at the end of Donkey Lane, which is one of my favourite suburban road names for no other reason than it makes me smile.

The design of the stadium is streamline moderne, with long horizontal lines and sweeping curves. It also has beautiful curved-steel Crittall windows that go on for miles. There are a very small number of surviving art deco stadiums in London, and even fewer streamline ones about, and it is Grade II listed for that very reason.

WEALDSTONE MOTORS
Pinner, HA2 6EH

Anyone who has ever driven through North Harrow will recognise this place immediately; it's very imposing, sitting as it does on a fork in the road.

It was originally built in 1933 at the end of a parade of suburban shops. Car showrooms were often built in a way that expressed modernity and speed, so were frequently designed in a streamline moderne style, with big, sweeping curves and neon lights. This one is a bit more reserved for the time, but nevertheless looks amazing today.

THE BROOKLANDS AERO CLUBHOUSE

Weybridge, KT13 0YP

In the 1910s, aviation became an increasingly popular hobby for the well off in London and the suburbs. Aerodromes sprang up in fields all around the city, including this clubhouse, which was built as a base for Brooklands flying school. Today, much of the old, banked Brooklands circuit is still there, and you can even walk on it without any restrictions if you wish.

BROCKWELL PARK LIDO
Herne Hill, SE24 0PA

One thing my nearest and dearest all know about me is that I really don't like indoor swimming pools. I hate the smell of chlorine, don't like the noise, and don't much like the feeling of the tepid water. But even I have to admit that a lido is a different proposition: I can sit in a deckchair with a cappuccino, look at some fab 1930s architecture and let the rest of the family get on with the unpleasant business of getting wet.

Come summertime, Brockwell Park Lido, like most of London's remaining lidos, is packed at the weekends from the moment it opens to the time the doors are finally closed. The day starts early, with eager people swimming lengths before they get on with the rest of their day. Those sporty types are soon replaced though, as hundreds of families turn up to enjoy a busy day of lazing in the sun, splashing around a bit and being shouted at for running by the pool.

However, lidos haven't always seen the love they deserve. In the 1960s, as the price of overseas holidays started to fall, people started to forgo a cold dip in the pool for sunny holidays abroad. Brockwell Park Lido itself was closed for four years until the community campaigned for it to reopen in the late 1990s.

CINEMAS

It might be hard to believe in a world dominated by at-home streaming services, but once upon a time, cinemas played a huge role in bringing people together. At first, they were small and poorly equipped, frequently little more than a projector and some raked seats in barrel-vaulted buildings or barns. But by the end of the 1930s, there were super cinemas in virtually every new estate, suburb and town – and wow, were they fancy!

After the Second World War, the economy boomed and all the major chains began competing for cinema-goers' hard-earned pennies. To give themselves an edge, cinemas often employed top architects to produce picture palaces

in the latest art deco and streamline moderne styles. Filled with state-of-the-art facilities, like ballrooms and restaurants, these designs were so iconic that they were seen all over the world, from LA to Calcutta.

Although a lot of these beautiful old buildings have been lost for ever, or no longer operate as cinemas, we still have just enough dotted around the suburbs to brighten our days when we come across them. You can pretty much guarantee that they'll be the fanciest building on the high street, even if they are more likely these days to house a kids' trampoline park or a chaotic indoor market.

THE ODEON
Balham, SW12 9EA

This building is what's left of the Balham Hill Odeon and was designed by renowned cinema architect George Coles for the legendary cinema owner and founder of the Odeon chain, Oscar Deutsch.

The original interior of the building had peach walls with silver accents, mahogany-and-walnut panels and stainless-steel balconies with sea-green rails.

The outside of the building was also an art deco extravaganza, with four horizontal lines of neon lights going right round the building and three going up that central fin.

About three years after it opened, the empty foyer was struck by a German bomb; however, as the auditorium was still intact, cinema-goers returned after a few weeks in true 'Keep Calm and Carry On'-style, and simply walked round the bomb damage to see the films.

The cinema closed in 1972, and in 1985 Majestic Wine moved in (and are still there), with notices announcing 'Britain's First Wine Cinema'. Today, only the original facade and foyer remain.

THE STATE CINEMA
Barkingside, IG6 2EF

This independent cinema was built in 1938 and is another picture house designed by George Coles. (Actually, almost all the cinemas in this section were designed by him! The man seemed to spend so much time designing cinemas that I wonder if he ever had time to relax in one and enjoy a film.)

The cinema was open for a grand total of two years before being hit by a bomb and was then requisitioned by the War Office to be used as a store house. It reopened in 1947 and passed through several different owners' hands before going into decline as TV took off.

Today, this cinema has been converted into a bingo hall – like a lot of other cinemas that have gone out of business. Not much has changed about this building though. In fact, if you go inside and look up from the lower floor, you'll see a false ceiling. Above that ceiling sits an abandoned balcony area that hasn't been touched since it closed in 1984, filled with dusty seats, faded curtains, cobwebs, flaking paint and a yellowing movie screen. It's funny to think, isn't it, that all of that is hidden above your head like some sort of huge, decaying time capsule?

THE GROSVENOR North Harrow, HA2 9TL

This building is the European headquarters of the Zoroastrian religion. In a former life it was a striking cinema, but with the decline of TV, the business was forced to close its doors.

I find the life cycle of old cinemas so fascinating: they all seem to open with so much pomp and fanfare in the 1930s, then get bought and sold time and again before going into decline. They usually reopen as bingo halls, then later, as the numbers of bingo-goers decline, they might become megachurches, like this one. Makes you wonder what the next phase of ownership will be, doesn't it?

THE ODEON Woolwich, SE18 6QQ

This huge ex-cinema sits on the south bank of the Thames and commands a very imposing position near the Woolwich Ferry. At the time of writing, it's a megachurch that you can hire out for weddings and corporate events. Grade II listed, it was one of the first art deco cinemas to be protected in this way, back in 1973.

THE ODEON Isleworth, TW7 4DH

This apartment block also used to be an Odeon – and in its heyday had bands of neon lights wrapped around the facade, later a signature feature of Odeon cinemas across the country.

It closed in 1957, just twenty-two years after opening, as an early casualty of the rise of TV.

THE GAUMONT STATE CINEMA
Kilburn, NW6 7HY

This dramatic-looking cinema dominates the skyline in Kilburn, North London. Opened in 1937, it was inspired by the Empire State Building, as you have no doubt spotted.

In addition to being a rather splendid cinema, the building immediately became one of London's premier music venues of the 1930s, and its opening concert, featuring Gracie Fields and George Formby, was broadcast live on BBC radio.

THE PICTUREHOUSE Bromley, BR1 1PQ

For most of its life, the fin-like structures on either side of this building were missing, but thanks to a refurbishment in 2016, Bromley Picturehouse looks stunning inside and out. It's one of the few art deco cinemas in the suburbs that's still open as a cinema – hurrah!

THE DOMINION Acton, W3 8QX

This lovely cinema in Acton was designed by Frank Ernest Bromage and opened in 1937 by Gracie Fields.

Now, an awful lot of old London cinemas are currently megachurches, having previously been bingo halls. If you've been wondering what the next stage is, the Dominion might have the answer. Today, it's a rock-climbing centre, adapted on the inside so that the artificial rock faces don't damage the walls of this Grade II listed building. This isn't a bad idea, I reckon. I've known a lot of rock climbers in my time, and the one thing they seem to have in common is a respect for the world around them (and skinny legs).

THE PREMIER ELECTRIC CINEMA
Turnpike Lane, N8 0QX

With all the grand cinemas you see in London, I thought it would be good to share a cute 'little' one for you, down a back street overlooking a green in North London.

It started life in 1910 as the Premier Electric Cinema and seated 900 people, all on one storey. It had a barrel-vaulted ceiling and a fancy Edwardian entrance whose diagonal roof line you might be able to just spot hidden behind the art deco facade, which was added in 1938. It has gone through multiple closures, reopening as a bingo club, then as an adult film cinema (which also showed Bollywood films at the weekend), then as a Laser Tag venue, then as a church, then as a cinema again, and is now a church once more. I feel bad for this place. The poor thing must be so confused by all the things that humans have asked it to be over the last hundred years or so! Still, it seems happy, down its side road overlooking the green, and the locals seem to love it.

THE WALPOLE PICTURE THEATRE
Ealing, W5 5BQ

Originally built in 1908 as a roller-skating rink, the Walpole was converted to a cinema in 1912. The auditorium was a huge, very basic, barrel-roofed shed, and the space was so tight that if a tall man was sitting in the back row, the shadow of his head would appear over the film being shown on the main screen.

The cinema was bought by Oscar Deutsch in 1936 and became an Odeon until its closure in 1972. When the building was demolished in 1981, the developers kept the tiled frontage and kind of glued it to the end of a house in Ealing, which is where you can see it today.

SUBURBAN ODDITIES

London's suburbs are peppered with things that either just don't seem to fit their environment and catch you by surprise or are ubiquitous to the point that we don't even notice them any more.

From remnants of the Victorian era to intriguing stuff created by today's artists and architects, it's great fun to spot these suburban peculiarities. They don't always make sense when you first see them, but there's often a fascinating story lurking behind their head-scratching presence.

THE MOSAIC HOUSE
Chiswick, London Borough of Hounslow

Known by locals as the Mosaic House, this eye-catching home is a labour of love by Carrie Reichardt, who inherited the building from her father.

Covered from top to bottom in thousands of ceramic tiles, each mosaic is firmly anti-establishment and depicts all sorts of humorous and political scenes. When she first moved in, the building had been covered in pebble-dash and, finding it hard to get her work accepted by the art world without making compromises, she began placing her mosaics on the outside of the house. Each mosaic reflects her mood and passions at the time, creating a huge scrapbook of her life.

There are always photographers outside, and since the rise of Instagram and TikTok, Carrie regularly sees people setting up equipment and creating all sorts of weird videos out there. She even woke up one day to find a group of Germans knocking at the door. It seems that Google had decided to list her home as a museum, and the tourists had been waiting in the street for the advertised opening time before knocking.

Turning the house into what it is

today has taken Carrie decades, but she didn't do it alone. To decorate the final part of the house, below the roof-line, she borrowed scaffolding from a friend which stayed up, mostly unused, for four years while her life took some dark twists and turns. Then one day, with her energy at a high again, she rallied a gang of thirty into finishing the whole thing with her. In two weeks the house was complete. In total, it took twenty years of work and four years of darkness under the scaffolding to complete the mosaics, and Carrie vividly remembers the moment the house was finished. With the scaffolding gone, light streamed into her home once more, and at that moment, with the vibrant colours of the entire house on display, Carrie said that she literally and metaphorically left the darkness and entered a world of light and colour.

Everyone from the neighbours to the council have been supportive of Carrie's project over the years, and she's well and truly accepted by the art world now. These days she gets commissioned to produce mosaics all over the world and regularly speaks at industry, community and school events.

THE HANWELL CLOCK TOWER
Hanwell, W7 3SP

This art deco clock tower was built to mark the coronation of George VI in 1937 and sits in the middle of Hanwell on what was probably the village square back in olden times but is a busy road junction today.

In the 1970s, a local estate agent vigorously campaigned to have the clock tower demolished, complaining that it was 'downright ugly'. Needless to say, he managed to strongly niggle the local community, who were very fond of it, and they responded to his demands to flatten the thing by raising the money to have it fully restored, which in Britain is the proper passive-aggressive response to someone who insults your clock tower. Upon seeing the sparkly clean tower and realising that the local community had stuck their collective two fingers up at him, he proclaimed, 'I admit having said some harsh things about its architectural inadequacies.' Incidentally, the name 'Hanwell' itself comes from the original Saxon, meaning 'stream frequented by cocks'. It's not clear if the estate agent in question frequented the stream, but I suspect he did.

THE SOUTHALL WATER TOWER
Southall, UB1 1QU

Of course, when the Queen complains about an eyesore, it's a different matter. Rumour has it that this railway water tower was built to look like a castle after Queen Victoria criticised the original, rather ugly design, calling it 'obscene' when she passed it on a train on the way to Windsor. What the Queen wants, she gets, and today this beautiful ex-water tower has been converted into housing.

THE MINIMAX FACTORY DOOR
Feltham, TW14 9ED

This piece of public art is a local landmark. Originally the entrance to a Minimax factory which produced fire extinguishers, it was so iconic among locals that the junction it sat on became known colloquially as the 'Minimax Corner'.

Today, a modern trading estate has sprung up around the gateway, but the old piece of art deco with its colourful ceramic tiles has remained, propped up by steel joists and wooden frames. It looks like the sort of thing that would have been vandalised and destroyed years ago, but the fact that it hasn't is quite heart-warming when you think about it.

THE HORNIMAN MUSEUM
Forest Hill, SE23 3PQ

  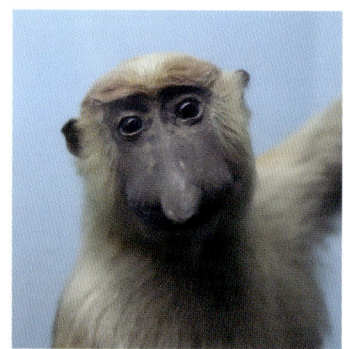

This is the Horniman Museum, which originally held the private collection of the heir of the world's biggest tea-trading company, Frederick Horniman. It houses a very Victorian collection of stuffed animals, as well as an aquarium, butterfly house and a host of other exhibits aimed at the twenty-first-century museum-goer.

It's a quirky place to visit, and my personal favourite item is the stuffed walrus. The skins were sent from Canada to a Victorian taxidermist who'd never seen one before – and they clearly didn't know that a walrus had saggy folds, so just kept stuffing it until the skin was tight, resulting in a sort of walrus bouncy castle.

PURLEY WAY DIVING BOARD
Croydon, CR0 4RQ

This is the diving board from Purley Lido, which was built opposite Croydon Airport in 1935. The lido closed in 1979 and only this beauty has survived. It's really hard to find it unless you know where to look: in an abandoned garden centre between a retail park and a hotel.

The pool itself opened with a swimming gala and a diving display from two Olympic gold medallists, and the guest of honour was the local mayor. On a poster advertising the event, the Olympic celebrities weren't named – though the mayor was. How times have changed!

The pool was 200 foot long by 70 foot, with a shingle beach and sunbathing lawns, and it was the first outdoor pool in the world with underwater lighting, heating and cleaning that were powered entirely by electricity.

BRAMBLE & MOSS
Richmond, TW10 6UB

This shop is currently a lovely florist's, but if you look closely at the doorstep you can see the word 'Blanchford' in mosaic, which refers to the pharmacy that originally sat here in the 1890s. Rex Blanchford's pharmacy was an interesting business that specialised in home-made miracle cures. The two he was most famous for were 'Jaborandi', a paraffin-based hair tonic that he sold using the long-lost Victorian marketing method of a badly written poem, and 'Khornout', a cure for corns. But the prize for the worst advert probably goes to one for 'Algine', which simply said: *Too fat! – Rex Blanchford's 'Algine' never fails to reduce weight: perfectly harmless.*

Would you trust a product that feels the need to assure you that it's 'perfectly harmless' when you didn't even ask?

PART 4

DAYS OUT OF THE SUBURBS

ROAD TRIP, ANYONE?

Contrary to what of a lot of us Londoners believe, there is life outside the huge circular car park that borders our city. It's a little different there – a cup of coffee isn't reassuringly expensive and strangers smile at you on the street – but take courage, it's well worth a visit and it's not as scary as it sounds.

This chapter features some of the iconic places and buildings that are within an hour or two of London, ones that maybe we visited as kids on a family day trip and that still strike nostalgia in us today.

BRIGHTON

There's a saying in Brighton that everyone seems to know and understand: 'No one from Brighton is from Brighton.' Of course, there are plenty of people who were born and grew up in this graceful seaside city, but a huge number of folks have moved there to make it their home, drawn to its bohemian and carefree vibe. I was one of those people in the 1990s, and for ten years I had the time of my life.

Brighton is all about the people and the atmosphere, and the architecture is just a vibrant backdrop for the cool things going on all around. For example, back in the 1990s, there was a whole bunch of secret codes for getting into the best nightclubs. If you were looking smart with shiny shoes, you had no chance of getting into the good clubs as they would clock that you were probably from out of town and maybe more interested in a punch-up than simply dancing until the sun came up and finding an all-night breakfast restaurant before showering and heading off to work.

Of course, it's still an awesome day out for visitors, with so much to do, be it donating your money to the amusements on the pier, shopping in the vintage clothes shops in North Laine or window-shopping in the dozens of jewellers crammed into the Lanes.

In the spirit of this book, I've picked a few things to look out for while walking (or Ubering) between your Brighton adventures.

If you're driving in from the north, you'll almost certainly be stuck in a jam near this building, which seems to have grown legs in a place where buildings don't usually grow legs. It's the Duke of York's Picturehouse, and claims to be one of the oldest continuously operating cinemas in the world, having opened in 1910.

Left: the former Savoy Cinema, turned casino
Opposite: Embassy Court

Just by the pier sits a very grand art deco building. Now a casino, the place was originally the Savoy Cinema and was opened in 1930 with a very modern innovation for the day: an underground car park. That'll never catch on!

If you keep walking west along the seafront until you get to the Hove Lawns, a very impressive building comes into view that seems a little out of place among all those Regency buildings. The sublime misfit that is Embassy Court was built in 1935 and was designed by superstar architect Wells Coates. It's always been seen as something a bit different and special – maybe that's why it was home to so many British celebrities from the 1930s to 1950s, such as music-hall legend Max Miller and actor Rex Harrison.

Sitting in the middle of Brighton, the Royal Pavilion (see over) was King George IV's seaside hangout. Building started in 1787 and over the years the design got more and more extravagant, leaving the city with a truly crazy building that is hard to ignore. The best time to see it in my humble opinion is over the Christmas period, when an outdoor ice rink appears on its lawns, the building is beautifully lit and the mulled wine flows freely.

If you walk along the beach westward towards Hove, you'll come across this resplendent Victorian bandstand. Although it was all but derelict from the 1970s, it was exquisitely restored in 2009 and live music is once again played from its platform in the summer months. There's something very romantic about this place. You can even get married here, although if you do you should expect a few seagulls to photo-bomb your wedding photos.

Opposite: the Royal Pavilion
This page: the Victorian bandstand

MARGATE

Margate was one of the first seaside towns frequented by Londoners even before the arrival of the railways, as it was reasonably easy to get to and from London by boat along the River Thames. From the 1920s to the 1960s, Margate boomed and a two-week holiday on the Kent coastline was something to look forward to each year, until things started to decline in the 1970s as flights got cheaper and holidaymakers began abandoning the UK for guaranteed sun in Europe.

I remember being taken to Margate on day trips as a kid. The Dreamland amusement park with its 1920s wooden roller coaster was the closest thing to Disneyland that our family could afford, and it was magical – even if a bloke had to sit in the middle of the roller-coaster train, pulling a brake lever as hard as he could to stop the train derailing. And of course, the wide sandy beaches were every bit as good as those of the South of France to me.

It's still a fun place to visit: those beaches haven't gone anywhere and back in 2002 the roller coaster was listed for preservation so it, along with the bloke with his hand on the brake, are still there. No one could ever say Margate is short of things to do or see!

You might recognise this building as the Empire Cinema from the 2022 Sam Mendes film, *Empire of Light*. It is, in fact, the Dreamland Cinema and has been closed since 2007. It's Grade II listed and thought to be the first cinema in the UK to feature the big fin-shaped thingy on the front that was very quickly copied by the Odeon chain.

To the west of the main beach area is the old, abandoned Lido (see over). There are still a few remnants of its former glory around, including this very art deco sign poking up above the promenade. It even lights up at night, which is very cool.

This page: the old Lido
Opposite: Droit House

The Droit House sits on the harbour arm, overlooking the main beach at Margate. Built in 1828, it was initially a customs office but was destroyed in the Second World War, only to be rebuilt from the original plans in 1947. These days it's a visitor centre with a neon sign above its entrance designed by local artist Tracey Emin.

WORTHING

I have to admit that when I lived in Brighton, I was heavily involved in the local pastime of ignoring Worthing altogether. The only time it ever seemed appropriate to mention the place was to complain about the traffic on its roundabout-infested bypass, so for a long time Worthing remained a place I'd heard of, but wasn't sure really existed (never mind the fact that it's just fourteen miles down the coast).

It was only when I went on a radical quest to discover if Worthing was real – much like that time I went to North London – that I realised the error of my ways. Worthing is flipping awesome! (The jury's still out on North London though . . . I jest!).

Worthing must be one of the UK's most elegant Georgian seaside towns. It's got a bit of a reputation for being a sleepy place where people go to retire, but constant development, particularly in the 1930s, has blessed it with some incredible buildings and a day out here is the perfect antidote to hectic city life. To give you a small flavour of just how lovely the buildings of Worthing are, the ones that follow can pretty much all be seen if you stand in a single spot by the seafront.

Worthing Pier was voted the Pier of the Year in 2019 and this is its Southern Pavilion, built in 1935 to replace the original structure that was destroyed in a fire. This building has been a nightclub, a cafe, a dance hall and even the home to a model railway. These days it's a delightful tea room and restaurant, with amazing views over the sea.

A super-cool amusement arcade (see over) sits in the middle of the pier. Built in the streamline moderne style in 1935, this is one of those buildings that makes you want to pull up a deckchair and just stare at it for a while.

Left: the former Pier Café
Opposite: the Dome Cinema

The Pavilion Theatre (see previous page) sits at the entrance to the pier and predates the other buildings there, having been built in 1926. It's still an entertainment venue but also hosts craft markets and fairs and is a top spot to grab breakfast if you're in town early enough.

Long ago, the above was called the Pier Café (as it's a cafe that overlooks the pier – who would have thought?). Back in the day it was a very 1930s affair, with huge, curvy steel windows wrapping around each of its three floors. It's still a restaurant, and you can get a very good idea of what it looked like back in its heyday by checking out those upper levels. Lovely!

The building on the right originally opened in 1911 as an amusement centre called the 'Kursaal', but converted to a cinema soon after. The name was changed to 'The Dome' in the First World War as 'Kursaal' sounded a bit German, which it is. It can refer to a recreation room at a spa, but was also widely used then as a term for an amusement park. It's still a gorgeous old cinema to this day.

SOUTHEND

Southend is one of those places I never went to as a kid because it was the place that East Londoners went to. The rules seemed to be that if you were from South London you went to Brighton, if you were from the East London you went to Southend, and if you were from South-East London you headed for Margate. I'm not sure those rules are written in stone anywhere, but it did rather seem like we were all allocated a seaside resort at birth. Goodness knows where people from North and West London ended up though – maybe they stayed at home?

Southend is a relative latecomer as a British seaside resort because for a long time the only way to get there was by stagecoach over poorly finished roads. In the early 1900s, the small town started to grow rapidly, not least thanks to the arrival of the railway. Soon attractions like the Kursaal – the world's first purpose-built amusement park – were built there, as well as Southend's famous pier, which is nearly a mile and a half long.

This page: the Kursaal
Opposite. Southend Cliff Lift and Sunray House, Westcliffe-on-Sea, in Southend's own suburbs

The Kursaal was the grand entrance to the fun park and contained a circus, ballroom, billiard hall and dining room. Since then, the building has seen its fair share of accidents and fires, and the attractions have changed over the years. At one point the ballroom was converted to a music venue, and for fans of AC/DC it is the Kursaal's stage that appears on the *Let There Be Rock* album cover.

Like Margate, Southend began to decline in the 1970s as the European package holiday gained popularity, and the outdoor amusement park and main building eventually closed.

Southend is having a bit of a renaissance though, with the fairly recent addition of the huge Adventure Island amusement park, which straddles the entrance to the pier. A long line of penny arcades graces the seafront, and in the summer it's full of excited kids trying to win cuddly toys out of the claw machines (and parents desperately trying to convince them that it's a waste of money).

This page: Axis Ride, Adventure Island

Opposite: penny arcades on the prom

BEKONSCOT MODEL VILLAGE
Beaconsfield, HP9 2PL

Bekonscot Model Village is a bit closer to London than the seaside destinations of Margate and Brighton and holds a special place in many of our hearts. It takes me back to a rare day out as a child with my grandparents, who were enchanted with the little model houses that were so reminiscent of their own childhoods.

It's the world's oldest surviving model village and started off as a private project in some bloke's back garden. Visiting it is one of the most British experiences you can have; not only does it seem like it's a tiny facsimile of suburbia, but it's got that marvellous home-made feel to it, from the moment you park at the village church opposite (it was never built as a tourist attraction, so doesn't have its own car park) to the friendly volunteers, the tea rooms situated in a large garden shed and the gentle puns on the names of the miniature-shop names, like Humpitt and Burnits' Coal Merchants.

It opened to the public in 1929 and has models of anything and everything that would have existed in the 1930s, all cheekily changed in the Bekonscot style – from the Hoovolux Factory to Hanton Court Palace. While newer models have been added over the years, a lot of care has been taken to display only buildings true to that era, so visiting feels a bit like time travelling – only you've grown really big in the process!

The nostalgia index is off the charts at Bekonscot, from the grandparents walking around reliving their memories of being taken there as children, to the happy suburban kids of today making new memories that no doubt they'll share with their own grandchildren one day. If there was one place in the world that was built to give you that warm, fuzzy feeling, it's Bekonscot Model Village. Nostalgia is what it used to be.

AND THAT'S A WRAP!

Well, dear reader, that concludes our little trip around London's suburbs (and some other exotic places too – aren't you lucky?). It's been a pleasure to explore the outskirts of this fine city, and I hope that you've enjoyed discovering – or even rediscovering – the suburbs with me.

As you may remember, I started my life in the suburbs feeling like I wanted to leave, to go somewhere more interesting. Now I realise that these areas are probably the most interesting part of any city, with true architectural masterpieces and funny characters around every corner. Every building has thousands of untold tales within its walls, and each one means something to so many of us, from the cinema where we had our first date to the factory that was always lit up at night on our way back from Grandma's house. More than just bricks and mortar, these buildings are bookmarks in the stories of our lives, stirring up memories and transporting us to moments we cherish. Because for many of us, suburbia is what we'll always call home.

Getting to meet my fellow suburbanites has been one of the best parts of writing this book, and I'd love to hear more from you. If you have any recommendations of new places to visit or days out of the suburbs, do join me on Instagram @LondonSuburbia and let's talk.

A BIG THANK-YOU FROM ME

So many people and organisations have inspired this book, but I would like to take the opportunity to single out a few of them here – thank you, you rock!

My kind and generous parents, Annette and Duncan, for the brilliant suburban childhood you gave Anna and me. We will never forget the safe and secure environment you created for us.

My crazy kids, Beth, Luke and Emily, who've had to endure my strange suburban obsession. I'm proud of you guys. You're amazing, creative and great fun to be around. Love you.

Jo, for allowing me the time to drive around all day with my camera, being weird, while you do all the hard work at home.

To the individuals who have offered help, advice, encouragement, inspiration and shared their knowledge freely, including Philip Butler, Lee Shelsher, John Clark, Sandy Weir, Philip Downer, Jack Fogg, Vanessa Phan, Helen Conford, Tony Lyons, Elle Taylor, Josh Abbott, Luke Agbaimoni, Mark Amies, all the lovely folk at the Art Deco Society UK, and Louis, the train guy.

All of the marvellous homeowners who have opened their doors, made me cups of tea, served me delicious cakes and allowed me to share their homes with you. To Miranda, Kevin & family, Ben & family, Paul & Jenny, Sharon & Andy, Marcus & Shereen, Julia & Adrian, Edward, Edward, Howard, Luciana & Sylvania, and Carrie.

And to the organisations who have agreed to share their buildings with us:

- **Bekonscot Model Village** • **The Horniman Museum** • **Transport for London**

And last but by no means least, thank you to all the wonderful friendly people of suburbia who I've met on the street while out taking these photos, and of course to all the people who talk to me every day on Instagram, who give me tips-offs about great buildings and who make me and others laugh with their fun and informative comments.

WANT TO EXPLORE SUBURBIA MORE?

BOOKS

If you want to find out more about the buildings in London's suburbia, you might like to invest in some of these excellent books. They're all written by experts in their fields, contain plenty of photos and would look great on your coffee table.

Abbott, Joshua	*Tube Station Anthology 1924–1961*, Art Deco Magpie, 2022
Abbott, Joshua	*Modernism in Metroland*, Unbound, 2020
Amies, Mark	*London's Industrial Past*, Amberley Publishing, 2020
Butler, Philip	*Odeon Relics*, Art Deco Magpie, 2019
Harwood, Elain	*Art Deco Britain*, B. T. Batsford Books, 2019
Schwartzman, Arnold	*London Art Deco*, Palazzo Editions Ltd, 2013
Tinniswood, Adrian	*The Art Deco House*, Mitchell Beazley, 2002
Various Authors	*London Suburbs*, Merrell Holberton Publishers, 1999
Yorke, F. R. S.	*The Modern House in England*, Architectural Press, 1937

ONLINE RESOURCES

While researching this book, I trawled the internet to find out more about the people and history behind the buildings featured. Here are some of my favourite websites:

britishnewspaperarchive.co.uk – a comprehensive online archive of newspapers stretching back to 1750.

cinematreasures.org – a massive database of cinemas past and present, including long-demolished picture houses.

findmypast.co.uk – a genealogy site that's great for finding out who lived at a certain address right up to 1939.

modernism-in-metroland.co.uk – an online guidebook that shows you where to find modernist buildings in the London suburbs.

Also, many local councils have a Local (heritage) List and Conservation Area Appraisals, which often go into great detail about the history of their local buildings and neighbourhoods.

GET INVOLVED

These societies are for all the lovers of art deco design and twentieth-century architecture – they're run by really cool and friendly people, and are a great way to get involved.

Art Deco Society UK: artdecosociety.uk – brings together lovers of art deco designs, covering everything from architecture to fashion. They run online and in-person events throughout the UK.

Twentieth Century Society: c20society.org.uk – this lot celebrate and save Britain's twentieth-century architecture and have been responsible for ensuring hundreds of buildings, including many in this book, are listed for preservation.

Boston Manor Station tower

ABOUT THE AUTHOR

Simon Pollock was born and raised in the suburbs of London. He started the Instagram account @LondonSuburbia in 2022. It began as a hobby and grew into a way to tell the overlooked stories of the people and buildings that make up 95 per cent of the city. In his spare time, he enjoys exploring exotic locations like Pinner, Chigwell, Bromley and Dagenham and has discovered that among the rows of 1930s semi-detached houses there are architectural marvels to rival South Beach in Miami. This is his first book.

1 3 5 7 9 10 8 6 4 2

Hutchinson Heinemann
20 Vauxhall Bridge Road
London SW1V 2SA

Hutchinson Heinemann is part of the Penguin Random House group of companies whose addresses can be found at global.penguinrandomhouse.com

Penguin Random House UK

Copyright © Simon Pollock, 2024

Simon Pollock has asserted his right to be identified as the author of this Work in accordance with the Copyright, Designs and Patents Act 1988

The author and publishers have made all reasonable efforts to contact copyright holders for permission, and apologise for any omissions or errors in the form of credit given. Corrections may be made in future reprints.

First published by Hutchinson Heinemann in 2024

www.penguin.co.uk

A CIP catalogue record for this book is available from the British Library

ISBN 9781529153958

Designed by Tony Lyons and Francesca Pike @ Estuary English

Printed and bound by Papercraft, Malaysia

The authorised representative in the EEA is Penguin Random House Ireland, Morrison Chambers, 32 Nassau Street, Dublin D02 YH68

www.greenpenguin.co.uk

Penguin Random House is committed to a sustainable future for our business, our readers and our planet. This book is made from Forest Stewardship Council® certified paper